AQA GCSE Modular Maths

Intermediate: Module 1

Trevor Senior and Gordon Tennant

Contents

D1350215

Pearson Education Limited
Edinburgh Gate
Harlow
Essex
CM20 2JE
England

www.longman.co.uk

First published 2003

ISBN   0 582 79593 1

Design and typesetting by Derek Lee

Printed in the U.K. by Scotprint, Haddington

The publisher's policy is to use paper manufactured from sustainable forests.

Acknowledgements

The publisher would like to thank Keith Gordon for his advice on the manuscript.

We are grateful for permission from the Assessment and Qualifications Alliance to reproduce past exam questions. All such questions have a reference in the margin. AQA can accept no responsibility whatsoever for accuracy of any solutions or answers to these questions. Any such solutions or answers may not necessarily constitute all possible solutions.

Introduction

AQA GCSE Modular Maths, Module 1 has been written by experienced examiners to help you get the most out of the handling data element of your Modular Mathematics course. This is the first text in a series of course books and revision resources that cover AQA Specification B at Intermediate Tier. This book can also be used to support the Handling Data element for other GCSE Mathematics courses.

Module 1 has four units, each split into several chapters. Unit 1, *Collecting, representing and interpreting data*, covers the initial collection, display and interpretation of data. Unit 2, *Diagrams for continuous data*, looks at diagrams that can be used to represent sets of data and how these diagrams can be used to analyse the data collected. Unit 3, *Processing data*, looks at the ways sets of data can be analysed through comparison and statistical calculations. Unit 4, *Probability*, looks at the probability of different types of events and the comparison between experimental and theoretical probabilities.

Each chapter has a short introduction followed by *worked examples*, *practice questions* and finally *practice exam questions*. Some of these are past exam questions (see note below). Answers are provided for all of the *practice* and *practice exam questions*. *Examiner tips*, located in the margins, give useful hints such as which topics may appear in the calculator and/or non-calculator section of the examination. The *reminders*, also located in the margin, give key knowledge already covered earlier and give references to other parts of the book. At the end of the book there is a practice exam paper with two sections (one calculator and one non-calculator) to help you prepare for the Module 1 exam.

You will also find this book useful when working on your Handling Data coursework task for Module 2. The first two units in the book, *Collecting, representing and interpreting data* and *Diagrams for continuous data*, cover the basics to get started on your Handling Data coursework.

Good luck in your exams!

Trevor Senior and Gordon Tennant

Note: Past exam questions are followed by a reference in the margin containing the year and awarding body that set them. All exam questions are reproduced with kind permission from the Assessment and Qualifications Alliance. Where solutions or answers are given, the authors are responsible for these. They have not been provided or approved by the Assessment and Qualifications Alliance and may not necessarily constitute the only possible solutions.

1 Questionnaires

A **questionnaire** or **survey** is a series of questions. They usually have a response section to record the answer for each question. You may be asked to design or criticise questions and response sections.

Questions

A question should follow these rules.

It should be:

- easy to understand
- easy to answer
- fairly brief.

It should not:

- be vague
- be **biased** or **leading**
- ask more than one question.

A question is thought to have bias or be leading if the answer or response is likely to be influenced by the way the question is written.

EXAMINER *TIP*

When you are asked to criticise a question you need to find a problem with it. This means that answering 'there is nothing wrong with it' will *not* get you any marks.

Example 1.1

Criticise this question.

'Do you agree that eating an unhealthy diet is bad for you?'

Solution

This is an example of a question that leads you to answer in a particular way or forces you to agree. Therefore the question shows bias.

There are two clear reasons why this question might lead you to agree with it.

- The phrase 'do you agree' suggests that agreeing is the correct response.
- The word 'unhealthy' suggests that this is not good for you.

Example 1.2

Criticise the questions below.

1 Do you have a computer and use it regularly?

2 Don't you agree that watching too much television is not good for you?

Solution

1 This asks two questions. You may not be able to answer it, e.g. if you have a computer but do not use it regularly. Also, different people will interpret the word 'regularly' in different ways, e.g. daily, weekly, etc.

2 This is a biased or leading question. 'Don't you agree' is attempting to force you to agree.

Response sections

Response boxes should follow these rules.

They should:

- be clear

- cover all possible answers.

They should *not*:

- have overlaps

- have too many choices.

When carrying out the survey it is also possible to receive biased responses. This can happen either because the questions are biased or leading, as in Example 1.2, or because the survey is given to people who might not be representative of the whole population. These are some examples of biased surveys:

- a survey about shopping that is carried out at a supermarket

- a survey about health and exercise that is carried out at a fitness centre

- a survey that only asks girls for their opinion

- a survey that only asks your friends.

You may be asked to criticise a survey. Your responses should state any obvious bias.

EXAMINER **TIP**

Don't just say 'biased'. Specify in which way the response is biased, e.g. 'biased towards car drivers'.

EXAMINER **TIP**

Do *not* say, 'they might not be telling the truth'.

Example 1.3

Criticise the response sections in the following questions.

1 How much do you earn in a day?

| | £0–20 | | £0–40 |
| | £40–50 | | More than £50 |

2 When do you use your computer?

| | Sometimes | | Occasionally |
| | Often | | Very often |

Solution

1 The £0–20 and £0–40 sections overlap, as someone earning £0–20 could tick the £0–40 box as well as the £0–20 box. £0–40 and £40–50 overlap because someone earning £40 could tick either the £0–40 box or the £40–50 box.

2 The words are vague. 'Sometimes' and 'occasionally' might mean the same thing to some people so they might tick more than one response box. You cannot answer 'never' because there is no response box for it.

Practice exam questions

1 Darren has written a questionnaire on smoking that he will use to collect
   data from other students at his sixth form college.

Smoking survey

Q1 What age were you when you started smoking?

☐ 10   ☐ 12   ☐ 14   ☐ 16   ☐ 18

Q2 How many cigarettes do you usually smoke each day?

☐ 0–1   ☐ 2–5   ☐ 5–10   ☐ 10–20   ☐ 20+

Write down one criticism of each question.   [AQA (SEG) 1998]

2 **a** Clare says, 'I go to the gym twice a week after school.' She decides to do
         a survey to investigate what exercise other pupils do outside school.
         Write down *two* questions that she could ask.

   b Matthew decides to do a survey in his school about the benefits of
         exercise. He decides to ask the girls' netball team for their opinion. Give
         two reasons why this is *not* a suitable sample to take.

   c This is part of Matthew's questionnaire.

Question	Don't you agree that adults who were sportsmen when they were younger suffer more from injuries as they get older?
Response	Tick one box
	☐ Yes ☐ Usually ☐ Sometimes ☐ Occasionally

---

   i   Write down *one* criticism of Matthew's question.

   ii Write down *one* criticism of Matthew's response section.   [AQA (NEAB) 2000]

2 Two-way tables

Two-way tables are tables that contain information about *two* different
variables. They allow you to access a large amount of information quickly. In
the exam, you may be asked to analyse or summarise information in a two-
way table.

Recording the makes of cars parked in a particular street would give a
frequency table for one variable.

Car make	Ford	Peugeot	Fiat	Mercedes	Citroen	BMW	Audi	Other
Frequency	12	5	2	1	2	3	1	8

You could also collect information on the colour of each of these cars and present the data in a two-way table. This table acts as an **observation sheet** to record data on two variables at the same time.

Make

		Ford	Peugeot	Fiat	Mercedes	Citroen	BMW	Audi	Other
	Red	II	I			I			IIII
	Black	III	III				II		I
	White		I						
Colour	Silver	I		I	I				
	Green			I			I	I	
	Blue	JHT				I			I
	Other	I							II

People often record data using a **tally** system. This involves grouping tallies into blocks of five to make them easier to count.

It is important that you use the tallies in blocks of five. We often use a **five bar gate** where four vertical tally marks are crossed out by a fifth diagonal tally mark.

JHT JHT III represents a total frequency of 5 + 5 + 3 = 13

Clear grouping of tallies into blocks of 5 is also acceptable: IIIII IIIII III

Once a tally chart has been completed the tallies should be counted; their respective frequencies should be transferred into a new table.

From this table you can now read off the frequency of each category, e.g. there are five blue Fords.

Make

		Ford	Peugeot	Fiat	Mercedes	Citroen	BMW	Audi	Other
	Red	2	1			1			4
	Black	3	3				2		1
	White		1						
Colour	Silver	1		1	1				
	Green			1			1	1	
	Blue	5				1			1
	Other	1							2

Example 2.1

Use the table on the previous page to answer the following questions.
In the survey:

a How many cars were there?

b How many blue cars were there?

c What is the most popular colour of car?

d What is the most popular make of car?

Solution

a Total each column and add the column totals together.

$12 + 5 + 2 + 1 + 2 + 3 + 1 + 8 = 34$

There were 34 cars in this survey.

b Add up the frequencies in the blue row.

$5 + 1 + 1 = 7$

There are seven blue cars in this survey.

c Count the number of cars for each colour. The colour with highest
frequency will be the most popular. The most popular colour of car in this
survey is black because there are nine black cars, which is more than any
other colour.

d In part a, you already found the total of each column. These totals are the
frequency of each make of car. The make of car with the highest frequency
is the most popular. In this survey, the most popular make of car is Ford
with a frequency of 12.

> *EXAMINER* **TIP**
> You could find the total for each
> row and then add the row totals
> together. Then check this answer
> by adding the column totals.

Example 2.2

This two-way table shows the numbers of visits made to the doctor and
the dentist by 80 students in the summer term.

Number of visits made to the doctor

		0	1	2	3
Number of visits made to the dentist	0	24	10	2	1
	1	8	5	3	1
	2	10	7	0	0
	3	5	3	1	0

a How many students did *not* visit the doctor?

b How many students visited the dentist exactly three times?

c How many students made more visits to the doctor than they made to the
dentist?

[AQA (SEG) 2000]

Solution

a The students who did *not* visit the doctor are shown in the *column* labelled 0. The sum of frequencies in this column is:

24 + 8 + 10 + 5 = 47

So 47 students did not visit the doctor.

b The students who visited the dentist exactly three times are those in the *row* labelled 3. The sum of the frequencies in this row is:

5 + 3 + 1 + 0 = 9

There are nine students who visited the dentist exactly three times.

c The students that made more visits to the doctor than the dentist are those in the top right-hand corner of the two-way table shown in green.

Number of visits made to the doctor

		0	1	2	3
Number of visits made to the dentist	0	24	10	2	1
	1	8	5	3	1
	2	10	7	0	0
	3	5	3	1	0

EXAMINER **TIP**

These 10 students made one visit to the doctor and zero visits to the dentist, so they made more visits to the doctor than they did to the dentist.

The sum of the green values is:

10 + 2 + 1 + 3 + 1 + 0 = 17

17 students made more visits to the doctor than they did to the dentist.

Example 2.3

A potato crisp manufacturer takes a sample of 20 packets of crisps from her factory. Their weights (in grams) are as follows.

25.88	25.51	26.01	25.25	25.40	26.15	25.70
25.82	26.19	25.63	26.02	25.98	25.94	25.70
25.68	25.45	25.61	25.83	25.91	25.68	

Complete the tally and the frequency columns in this table.

Weights (grams)	Tally	Frequency
25.20 to less than 25.40		
25.40 to less than 25.60		
25.60 to less than 25.80		
25.80 to less than 26.00		
26.00 to less than 26.20		

[AQA (SEG) 1997]

9

Solution

This data is continuous (it can take any value in a range) and you have to be careful that you allocate a tally to the correct class interval. The ideal way is to cross out each value in pencil and insert a tally mark in the correct class interval, e.g. 25.88 lies in the class interval 25.80 to 26.00 and so you insert a tally mark in that class interval.

Weights (grams)	Tally	Frequency
25.20 to less than 25.40	I	1
25.40 to less than 25.60	III	3
25.60 to less than 25.80	ЖНТ I	6
25.80 to less than 26.00	ЖНТ I	6
26.00 to less than 26.20	IIII	4

> **Reminder**
> Use the five bar gate when tallying.

> **EXAMINER TIP**
> Always check that the total frequency matches the amount of data that you were given.

Practice questions

1 Geeta is carrying out a survey at her college. She asked 50 students how much they earned last week from their part-time jobs. These are the last 10 replies.

£15.50   £12.50   £0.00   £10.00   £24.80
£18.00   £17.50   £15.00   £35.00   £49.00

a Copy the table and add these results to the 40 tallies already on the tally sheet and then complete the frequency column.

Amount earned (£)	Tally	Frequency
0.00 to 9.99	ЖНТ ЖНТ ЖНТ	
10.00 to 19.99	ЖНТ ЖНТ ЖНТ II	
20.00 to 29.99	IIII	
30.00 to 39.99	III	
40.00 or over	I	

b Use your frequency column to write down the modal class of the amount earned.

Geeta gave out a short questionnaire which contained the following question:

'How many hours did you work?'

c Write down two criticisms of this question.

> **Reminder**
> The modal class is the class with the highest frequency.

[AQA (SEG) 1997]

2 Four taxi drivers recorded how many passengers they carried on each journey during one evening. The table shows the numbers of journeys they made with each different number of passengers.

Number of passengers carried

		1	2	3	4
	A	6	6	4	0
	B	7	7	3	1
Taxi	C	5	7	2	0
	D	4	4	3	1

For example, taxi C had five journeys for which there was only one passenger.

a Which taxi completed the most journeys that evening?

b Calculate the total number of journeys where exactly three passengers were carried.

c There were 60 journeys made altogether. Calculate the total number of passengers that were carried on these 60 journeys.

[AQA (SEG) 1999]

Practice exam question

1 A factory manager asked each of his 36 employees how many cups of tea and cups of coffee they drank at work yesterday. The results are shown in the two-way table.

Number of cups of tea

		0	1	2	3
	0	0	3	7	2
Number of cups of coffee	1	4	2	3	1
	2	5	3	2	0
	3	0	1	2	1

a How many employees drank two cups of tea?

b How many employees drank the same number of cups of tea as cups of coffee?

c How many employees drank more cups of tea than cups of coffee?

d Calculate the total number of cups of tea drunk by the employees.

[AQA (SEG) 2001]

3 Pie charts

A **pie chart** is a circle split into **sectors** where each sector represents a category from a set of data. The size of the angle in each sector is proportional to the **frequency** of the category as a fraction of the **total frequency**.

Pie charts are used to represent **categorical** data such as eye colour or different sporting activities. These are sets of data that cannot be measured on a continuous scale.

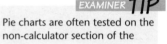
EXAMINER *TIP*

Pie charts are often tested on the non-calculator section of the exam.

Drawing a pie chart

To draw a pie chart to represent a set of data you have to calculate the angle for each sector. The sum of the angles for each of the sectors is 360°. You use this to calculate the angle for each category.

$$\text{Angle of a sector} = \frac{\text{category frequency}}{\text{total frequency}} \times 360°$$

Example 3.1

At a college, each student chose an activity to do on Wednesday afternoons. The table shows how many students chose each activity.

Activity	Number of students	Angle (°)
Sport	380	
IT	280	
Community work	100	
College magazine	40	
Total		

A pie chart is to be drawn to represent the data.

a Calculate the angle for the sector that represents Sport.

b Draw and label a pie chart to represent the data.   [AQA (SEG) 1999]

Solution

a First calculate the total frequency. Then divide the frequency for Sport by the total frequency and multiply by 360°.

Total frequency = 380 + 280 + 100 + 40 = 800

Angle for Sport sector:

$$\frac{\text{category frequency}}{\text{total frequency}} \times 360° = \frac{380}{800} \times 360°$$

$$= 171°$$

b To draw the pie chart you have to calculate the angles for the other sectors.

IT: Community work: College magazine:

$$\frac{280}{800} \times 360° = 126°$$ $$\frac{100}{800} \times 360° = 45°$$ $$\frac{40}{800} \times 360° = 18°$$

Check that the angles add up to 360°. If they do, then use the angles to draw the pie chart. If not, go back and check your working.

To draw the pie chart use a protractor and a ruler to draw the sectors accurately.

Make sure each sector in the pie chart is clearly labelled. If you have time to colour the sectors you can use a **Key**, if not then write the labels inside the sectors. (Both options are shown below.)

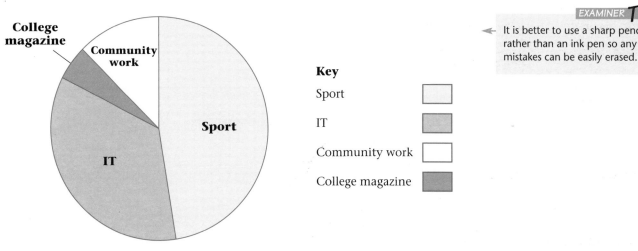

> EXAMINER *TIP*
>
> It is better to use a sharp pencil rather than an ink pen so any mistakes can be easily erased.

Key

Sport

IT

Community work

College magazine

Example 3.2

Draw a pie chart to represent this data.

Favourite fish	Number of people	Angle (°)
Cod	9	
Haddock	5	
Plaice	7	
Other	3	
Total	24	360°

> EXAMINER *TIP*
>
> The frequencies of the categories in exam questions usually add up to a factor of 360 (e.g. 30 or 36) or to a number where scaling can be used (e.g. 240).

Solution

In a pie chart, the total frequency is represented by 360°. Here the total frequency is 24 people. Find the size of the angle that represents a single person by dividing 360° by 24.

$$\frac{360°}{24} = 15°$$

Calculate the size of the angle for each category by multiplying the number of people in the category by 15°.

Cod: $9 \times 15° = 135°$ Plaice: $7 \times 15° = 105°$

Haddock: $5 \times 15° = 75°$ Other: $3 \times 15° = 45°$

Put your working in the extra columns in the table.

Favourite fish	Number of people	Angle (°)
Cod	9	$\frac{360}{24} \times 9 = 135$
Haddock	5	$\frac{360}{24} \times 5 = 75$
Plaice	7	$\frac{360}{24} \times 7 = 105$
Other	3	$\frac{360}{24} \times 3 = 45$
Total	**24**	**360**

EXAMINER **TIP**

Check that all the angles add up to 360°.

Draw a circle and mark the centre. Then measure out the angles of the sectors and draw in the lines to mark them.

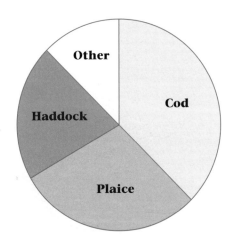

EXAMINER **TIP**

Each sector must be drawn to within 2° of the correct angle and labelled correctly.

Example 3.3

Draw a pie chart to represent this data.

Colour	Frequency	Angle (°)
Red	140	
Blue	60	
Yellow	30	
Green	10	
Total	**240**	**360**

Solution

If you multiply the total frequency (240) by 1.5 it equals 360°. So to find the size of each individual angle, multiply the frequency of the category by 1.5.

Colour	Frequency	Angle (°)
Red	140	140 × 1.5 = 210
Blue	60	60 × 1.5 = 90
Yellow	30	30 × 1.5 = 45
Green	10	10 × 1.5 = 15
Total	240	360

Reminder
Check that all the angles add up to 360°.

Use the calculated angles to draw the pie chart.

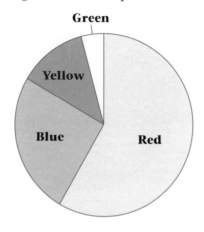

Interpreting a pie chart

Questions about pie charts often involve fractions or percentages, so it is useful to remember some basic fractions and percentages of 360°.

90° is $\frac{1}{4}$ or 25% of 360°.   120° is $\frac{1}{3}$ or 33% of 360°.

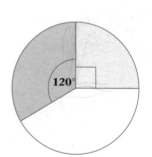

Example 3.4

Belinda says, 'A is twice as big as B'.

Explain how you could show that she is correct.

Solution

Measure the angles to see whether the angle for sector A is twice as large as the angle for sector B.

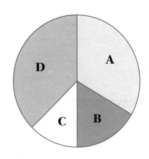

Practice questions

1 Draw pie charts to represent the following sets of data.

a The favourite subject of year 10 pupils.

Subject	Maths	Science	French	English	Art
Frequency	6	7	3	4	4

b The different colours of people's bedrooms.

Subject	Blue	Red	Green	Yellow	Other
Frequency	3	9	1	2	3

2 The pie chart shows different animals on a farm. Look at the pie chart and state whether the following statements are true or false. Give reasons for your answers.

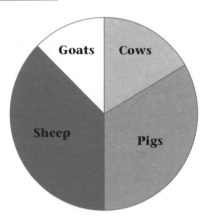

a The probability that an animal picked at random is a pig is $\frac{1}{3}$.

b There are more cows and goats than sheep.

c There are twice as many cows as goats.

d More than half the animals are sheep and goats.

Practice exam questions

1 The table shows items that were sold by a shop in the month of October. A pie chart is to be drawn to represent the data.

a Calculate the angles for each sector and insert them into the Angle column in the table.

Item	Value (£)	Angle (°)
Umbrellas	350	
Wellington boots	560	
Gloves	123	
Hats	155	
Scarves	72	
Total		

b Draw a pie chart to represent this data.

[AQA (SEG) 1998]

2 The table shows the average daily water use for a typical family of four people.

Water use	Amount (litres)	Angle (°)
Baths and showers	90	
Washing machine	66	
Flushing toilet	174	
Other	210	
Total		

Draw a pie chart to represent this data.   [AQA (SEG) 1997]

4 Averages

The **mean**, **median**, and **mode** are all different types of **average**. Throughout the exam you will asked to calculate the mean, median and mode for sets of data.

The mode

The mode is the most common value in a set of data.

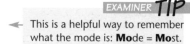

EXAMINER **TIP**

◄— This is a helpful way to remember what the mode is: **Mo**de = **Mo**st.

Example 4.1

Write down the mode for this set of numbers.

8   7   6   1   7   7   6   5   2

Solution

To find the mode, look for the number that occurs the most.

8 ⑦ 6   1 ⑦ ⑦ 6   5   2

EXAMINER **TIP**

◄— With larger sets of data it is helpful to order the data.

Seven occurs more times than any other number.

Mode = 7

The median

The median is the middle value of a set of data when the data has been sorted into order of size.

To find the position of the median you can use this formula.

Median position = $\dfrac{n+1}{2}$ where n is the number of pieces of data.

Example 4.2

Work out the median for this set of numbers.

4   7   4   8   6   6   4   10   2

Solution

First of all the numbers need sorting into order of size.

2   4   4   4   6   6   7   8   10

Median position is $\dfrac{9 + 1}{2} = 5$

The position of the median is the fifth value.

Count along the set of data to the fifth value; this is the median.

2   4   4   4   (6)   6   7   8   10

The median = 6

If the data contains an even number of values, there will be two values in the middle when the data has been sorted into order of size. In this case, the median is halfway between these two middle values.

Example 4.3

Work out the median for this set of numbers.

4   8   3   6   4   4   3   7   9   12

Solution

Put the numbers into order by size.

3   3   4   4   4   6   7   8   9   12

Median position is $\dfrac{n + 1}{2} = \dfrac{10 + 1}{2} = 5.5$

So the median is halfway between the fifth and sixth values.

3   3   4   4   (4)(6)   7   8   9   12

The median is halfway between 4 and 6. Median = 5

The mean

The mean of a set of data is the sum of all the data divided by the number of pieces of data.

Example 4.4

Work out the mean of this set of numbers.

6   8   7   1   7   5   4   0

EXAMINER **TIP**

This is a helpful way to remember what the median is: **Med**ian = **Mid**dle.

EXAMINER **TIP**

This is a helpful way of remembering what the mean is: Me**an** = **A**dd 'n' divide.

Solution

The sum of the data is: $6 + 8 + 7 + 1 + 7 + 5 + 4 + 0 = 38$

There are eight pieces of data.

Mean $= \dfrac{38}{8} = 4.75$

The mean for this set of data is 4.75. Note that the mean does not always work out to be an exact number in the set of data.

The range

The range is a measure of the spread of a set of data. It can be worked out using the following formula.

Range = largest value – smallest value

Example 4.5

What is the range of this set of data?

5   8   1   9   3   4   6   8

Solution

First order the set of data by size.

(1)   3   4   5   6   8   8   (9)

Range = 9 – 1 = 8. The range for this set of data is 8.

Practice question

1 Work out the mode, median, mean and range for the following sets of data.

    a 3   11   5   4   5   6   7   14   8   **b** 6   4   6   1   3   6   13   2   4

    c 4   8   6   5   7   10   3   5   **d** 6   6   3   5   7   9   3   3

> EXAMINER *TIP*
> Learn a way of remembering each type of average. A common mistake in exams is to work out the wrong one.

Practice exam questions

1 The lateness of 12 trains is recorded. The results (in minutes) are shown.

−1   1   2   2   3   3   3   5   6   6   9   15

    a What is the range in lateness?   **b**   What is the mean lateness?   [AQA (SEG) 1999]

2 Five boys run a 200 metre race. Their times are shown in the table.

Name	Andy	Boris	Chris	Darren	Eric
Time (seconds)	25.0	23.4	26.1	22.8	24.2

What is the median time?   [AQA (NEAB) 2002]

5 Stem and leaf diagrams

Stem and leaf diagrams are used to show how sets of data are distributed. An ordered stem and leaf diagram can be used to calculate statistics such as the range, median and the interquartile range.

Forming a stem and leaf diagram

Stem and leaf diagrams are like horizontal bar charts where the axis is the stem and the last digits of the numbers are the leaves that form the bars.

Here is a set of **discrete** data.

14   19   27   16   21   10   32   29   19   10   17   19   33   22   24

Discrete data can only take certain values, in this case whole numbers.

This data can be collected into three categories and sorted into ascending order.

Numbers from 10 to 19	10	10	14	16	17	19	19	19
Numbers from 20 to 29	21	22	24	27	29			
Numbers from 30 to 39	32	33						

Now the ordered stem and leaf diagram is formed. This is done by putting the numbers representing the tens in the left-hand column, and putting their corresponding ordered units in the right-hand columns. A key is given to show what the diagram means.

KEY: 2 | 4   represents 24

```
1 | 0  0  4  6  7  9  9  9
2 | 1  2  4  7  9
3 | 2  3
```

Interpreting a stem and leaf diagram

The stem and leaf diagram above has 15 pieces of data. The diagram can be used to find the range, the median and the interquartile range of this data.

The range

The range is the difference between the largest and the smallest values in a set of data. In this diagram the largest value is 33 and the smallest value is 10.

KEY: 2 | 4   represents 24

```
1 | 0  0  4  6  7  9  9  9
2 | 1  2  4  7  9
3 | 2  3
```

Range is 33 – 10 = 23

The median

The median is the middle value when the data is arranged in ascending order.

In the following diagram, there are 15 pieces of data. Use the formula to find the position of the median provided the data is in order of size.

Reminder
To calculate the position of the median use this formula:
$\frac{(n+1)}{2}$ where n is the number of values in the set of data.

Position of the median is $\dfrac{(15+1)}{2} = 8$

In this stem and leaf diagram the median is the eighth value.

KEY: 2 | 4   represents 24

```
1 | 0  0  4  6  7  9  9  ⑨
2 | 1  2  4  7  9
3 | 2  3
```

Median = 19

Quartiles

Sets of data can be split into four equal sections divided by three quartiles. You can use the stem and leaf diagram to find the value of the quartiles. The **lower quartile** is the value that is $\frac{1}{4}$ of the way through the data when arranged in ascending order. To calculate the position of the lower quartile use this formula:

$\dfrac{(n+1)}{4}$ where n is the number of values in the set of data.

Position of the lower quartile is $\dfrac{(15+1)}{4} = 4$

Use the stem and leaf diagram to count along to the lower quartile, which in this case is the fourth value.

KEY: 2 | 4   represents 24

```
1 | 0  0  4  ⑥  7  9  9  9
2 | 1  2  4  7  9
3 | 2  3
```

Lower quartile = 16

The **upper quartile** is the value that is $\frac{3}{4}$ of the way through the data when arranged in ascending order. To calculate the position of the upper quartile use this formula:

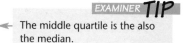

EXAMINER **TIP**
The middle quartile is the also the median.

$\dfrac{3(n+1)}{4}$ where n is the number of values in the set of data.

Position of the upper quartile is $\dfrac{3(15+1)}{4} = 12$

Use the stem and leaf diagram to count along to the upper quartile, which in this case is the 12th value.

KEY: 2 | 4   represents 24

```
1 | 0  0  4  6  7  9  9  9
2 | 1  2  4  ⑦  9
3 | 2  3
```

Upper quartile = 27

The interquartile range

The **interquartile range** is a measure of the spread of a set of data. To calculate the interquartile range, use this formula:

Interquartile range = upper quartile – lower quartile

Use the values found for the quartiles to calculate the interquartile range.

Interquartile range is 27 – 16 = 11

Example 5.1

Here are the test scores for 11 pupils.

13   17   9   21   25   17   19   20   25   7   9

a Complete the stem and leaf diagram.

EXAMINER **TIP**

KEY: ... | ... represents 13 ← Remember to complete the key.

```
0 |
1 |
2 |
```

b How many pupils scored more than 10?

c What was the median score?

d An extra pupil takes the test and scores 25. What is the new median?

Solution

a   KEY: 1 | 3   represents 13

```
0 | 7  9  9
1 | 3  7  7  9
2 | 0  1  5  5
```

b   KEY: 1 | 3   represents 13

```
0 | 7  9  9
1 | 3  7  7  9
2 | 0  1  5  5
```

The rectangle shows the scores greater than 10.

8 pupils scored more than 10.

c   KEY: 1 | 3   represents 13

```
0 | 7  9  9
1 | 3  7  ⑦  9
2 | 0  1  5  5
```

Position of the median score is $\dfrac{11 + 1}{2} = 6$

The median is the sixth value on the stem and leaf diagram.

Median = 17

d Add the extra pupil's score to the stem and leaf diagram (it can go on the end of the third row as no pupils scored higher than 25). Calculate the new position of the median and use it to find the value of the new median.

Position of the new median is $\dfrac{12 + 1}{2} = 6.5$

The value of the new median is the mean of the sixth and seventh values.

New median is $\dfrac{17 + 19}{2} = 18$

Practice questions

1 The number of passengers using a school bus is recorded over two weeks. Here are the results.

53   37   41   41   39   45   37   48   51   42

a Copy and complete the stem and leaf diagram.

KEY: ... | ... represents ... passengers

```
3 |
4 |
5 |
```

b What is the range of the data?

2 The stem and leaf diagram below represents the number of fish caught by 15 fishermen on one day.

KEY: 1 | 3   represents 13 fish

```
0 | 0  0  0  0  0  1  2  5
1 | 3  3  3  6  7
2 | 2  5
```

Use the stem and leaf diagram to find the following:

a the range

b the mode

c the median

d the interquartile range.

Another fisherman catches six fish on one day.

e If this data is included in the stem and leaf diagram will the median increase, decrease or stay the same? Explain your answer.

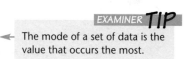

EXAMINER TIP

◄— The mode of a set of data is the value that occurs the most.

3 The number of people queuing at a town's main post office each lunchtime is recorded below.

11   15   2   20   18   16   20   9   10   19   22   21   14   11

8   4   12   23

a Copy and complete the stem and leaf diagram, including the key, to represent the data.

KEY: ... | ...   .

```
0 | ...............
1 | ...............
2 | ...............
```

b The number of people queuing at a bank at lunchtime each day is shown in the ordered stem and leaf diagram below.

KEY: 1 | 3   represents 13

```
0 | 1  1  2  3  3  4  4  5  6  8
1 | 0  1  2  3  5
2 | 1
```

Use the ordered stem and leaf diagram to find the median number of people queuing at the bank at lunchtimes.

Practice exam question

1 The stem and leaf diagram shows the test scores of some pupils.

KEY: 4 | 3   means a score of 43

```
0 | 9
1 | 0  2  2  6  7  8
2 | 0  3  3  5  6
3 | 2  7
4 | 3
```

a How many pupils scored less than 15?

b What was the median score?

c An extra pupil takes the test and scores 29. Add this score to the stem and leaf diagram and find the new median score.

[AQA 2002]

6 Frequency diagrams

A **frequency diagram** is a graph or chart that shows the frequencies of sets of data. In the exam, you could be asked to draw a **histogram** or a **frequency polygon**.

EXAMINER **TIP**

If you are asked to draw a frequency diagram, you can choose to draw a histogram or a frequency polygon.

Histograms

A histogram is a frequency diagram that is used to display **continuous** data. Continuous data is data that can take any value within a given range, e.g. the lifetime of a battery.

The data collected is separated into **class intervals**. A class interval is a section of the range of data. If we consider data collected for the lifetime of a battery, one class interval might be $0 \leqslant t < 1$ hours. All the times that are greater than or equal to 0 hours but less than 1 hour are recorded in this class interval.

EXAMINER **TIP**

In the exam, the class intervals will always be the same size.

Drawing a histogram

To draw a histogram you need to draw out the horizontal and vertical axes. In the exam they are usually drawn for you. The horizontal axis shows the boundaries of the class intervals. The vertical axis shows the frequency. For each class interval a bar is drawn. There should be no gaps between the bars.

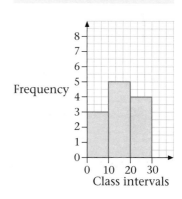

Example 6.1

The lengths of 20 TV programmes are shown in the table.

Length, l (minutes)	Number of TV programmes
$20 \leqslant l < 30$	8
$30 \leqslant l < 40$	5
$40 \leqslant l < 50$	3
$50 \leqslant l < 60$	4

Use the data to draw a histogram.

Solution

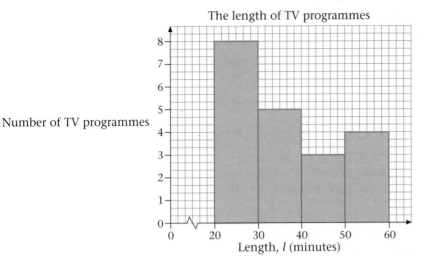

Although it looks similar to a bar chart, there are two important differences:

● the scale is continuous

● there are no gaps between the bars.

Frequency polygons

A frequency polygon is a line graph made from a histogram. The frequency of each class interval is plotted at the mid-point of that class interval and the points are joined by straight lines. Frequency polygons are mainly used for looking at the shape of a distribution or for comparing two sets of data.

Drawing a frequency polygon

To draw a frequency polygon you need to calculate the mid-point of each class interval, e.g. for the interval $20 \leqslant l < 30$ the mid-point is 25.

Then plot the frequencies against the mid-point for each class. Finally join the points with straight lines using a ruler.

Example 6.2

a Calculate the mid-points of the following class intervals.

b Use the mid-points to draw the frequency polygon.

Length, *l* (minutes)	Number of TV programmes	Class mid-point
$20 \leqslant l < 30$	8	
$30 \leqslant l < 40$	5	
$40 \leqslant l < 50$	3	
$50 \leqslant l < 60$	4	

Solution

a First calculate the mid-points for each class interval. Sometimes you will be able to see the mid-point just by looking at the upper and lower boundaries of the class. If not, then use this formula:

$$\text{Mid-point} = \frac{\text{Lower boundary} + \text{Upper boundary}}{2}$$

Length, l (minutes)	Number of TV programmes	Class mid-point
$20 \leqslant l < 30$	8	25
$30 \leqslant l < 40$	5	35
$40 \leqslant l < 50$	3	45
$50 \leqslant l < 60$	4	55

b Use the mid-points to draw the frequency polygon. The horizontal axis shows the mid-points and the vertical axis shows the frequency. The points are joined by straight lines.

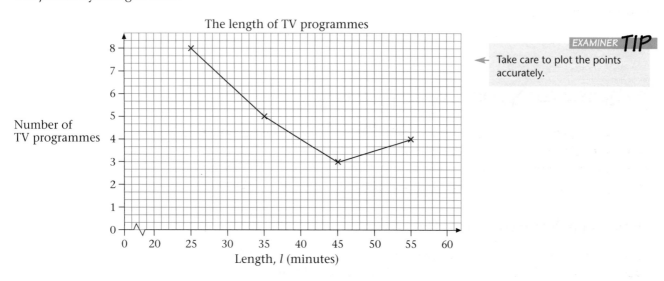

EXAMINER **TIP**

Take care to plot the points accurately.

Practice questions

1 A postwoman kept a record of the mass of each of the parcels posted in one day. The following table shows the results.

Mass (kg)	Frequency
Up to and including 1	7
More than 1 and less than or equal to 2	12
More than 2 and less than or equal to 3	6
More than 3 and less than or equal to 4	5
More than 4 and less than or equal to 5	3

Draw a histogram to represent the data.

2 The table shows the time spent in a single visit to a burger bar by 30 teenagers.

Time spent	Frequency
5 minutes or more but less than 10 minutes	4
10 minutes or more but less than 15 minutes	8
15 minutes or more but less than 20 minutes	9
20 minutes or more but less than 25 minutes	6
25 minutes or more but less than 30 minutes	3

Draw a frequency polygon to represent the data.

3 A manufacturer of bottles of tomato sauce measures the weights of 20 samples from the factory. The weights (in grams) are as follows.

450.3   452.6   457.1   451.8   452.5   456.4   450.2   453.6   458.2   450.6
454.4   455.9   450.1   452.7   450.9   453.6   457.2   456.0   451.9   455.0

Weight (g)	Tally	Frequency
450 to less than 452		
452 to less than 454		
454 to less than 456		
456 to less than 458		
458 to less than 460		

a Copy the table and complete the tally and the frequency columns.

b Draw a frequency polygon to represent the data.

c The weight printed on the bottles is 450 grams. Comment on whether you think that the manufacturer will be satisfied with the results.

EXAMINER TIP
You can say that the manufacturer is satisfied or dissatisfied with results as long as you justify your answer using the given data.

Practice exam questions

1 The amount of time spent by a group of pupils on their mobile phones in one week is recorded. Here are the results.

Time	Number of pupils
Less than 10 minutes	12
10 minutes or more but less than 20 minutes	9
20 minutes or more but less than 30 minutes	13
30 minutes or more but less than 40 minutes	6
40 minutes or more but less than 50 minutes	8
50 minutes or more but less than 60 minutes	2

a State the modal class.

b Copy and complete the histogram.

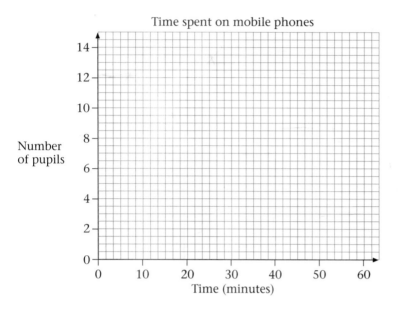

Time spent on mobile phones

[AQA (NEAB) 2001]

2 The table shows the length of some cinema films.

Length, l (min)	Number of films
$80 < l \leqslant 100$	10
$100 < l \leqslant 120$	3
$120 < l \leqslant 140$	6
$140 < l \leqslant 160$	1

Copy the graph and use the information to draw a frequency polygon.

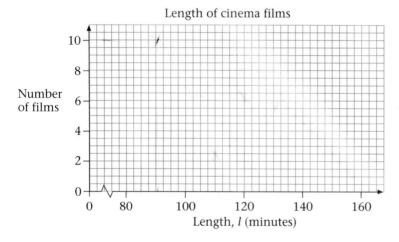

Length of cinema films

[AQA 2002]

7 Line graphs (time series)

A **line graph** is used to compare two variables by plotting points on a graph and joining the points with straight lines. In the exam, you will be asked questions about a special type of line graph called a **time series** graph.

Time series graphs are line graphs with time as the variable on the horizontal axis. These graphs show how a variable moves or changes with time.

For example, a car driver or a train driver will change their speed in the course of a journey. So, on a graph showing the changes of speed, speed will be the variable on the vertical axis and time will be on the horizontal axis.

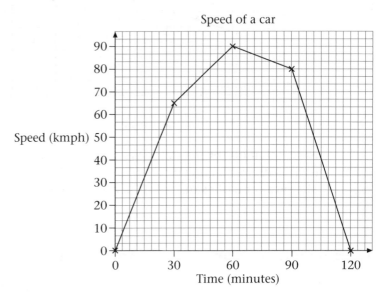

Drawing a time series graph

To draw a time series graph you plot points of one variable against time onto a graph. These points are then joined by straight lines.

Example 7.1

A baby's weight was monitored in its first six weeks. The weights of the baby at different times are shown in the table.

Time (weeks)	Weight (lbs)
1	7.8
2	8.2
3	8.5
4	9.0
5	9.4
6	9.9

Use the table to plot a time series graph.

Solution

The points are plotted and then joined using straight lines.

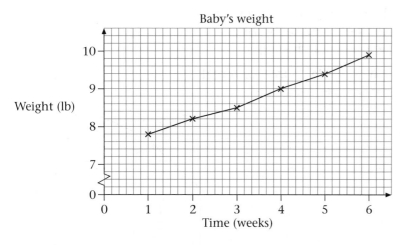

Notice that on the graph the vertical axis starts at 0 and then jumps to 7. There is a zig-zag line between 0 and 7. This is called a **break**. The break squashes the values between 0 and 7.

Reading values from a time series graph

Once you have plotted a graph you may be asked to read certain values from it.

Example 7.2

Use your graph in Example 7.1 to estimate the baby's weight after 4.5 weeks.

Solution

Go along the Time axis to 4.5 weeks and draw a vertical line up to meet the straight line segment on the graph. Then draw a horizontal line across from that point to meet the vertical axis. Where your line cuts the vertical axis shows the baby's weight after 4.5 weeks (about 9.2 lbs).

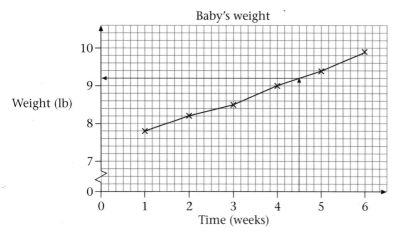

Practice questions

1 Draw time series graphs of the following data.

a

Quarters	Q1, 2001	Q2, 2001	Q3, 2001	Q4, 2001	Q1, 2002	Q2, 2002	Q3, 2002
Gas bill (£)	105	85	49	68	120	90	52

b

Time	8 am	10 am	12 pm	2 pm	4 pm	6 pm	8 pm
Temperature (°C)	18	24	28	30	25	20	16

Practice exam questions

1 A weather forecaster recorded the hourly temperature on one afternoon in December.

Time	12 pm	1 pm	2 pm	3 pm	4 pm
Temperature (°C)	4	5	4.5	3.5	3

a Draw a line graph to represent the data.

b i Use your line graph to estimate the temperature at 2.15 pm.

ii Explain why your answer can only be an estimate.   [AQA (SEG) 1997]

2 The following graph appeared in a newspaper advert. Write down two ways in which the graph is misleading.

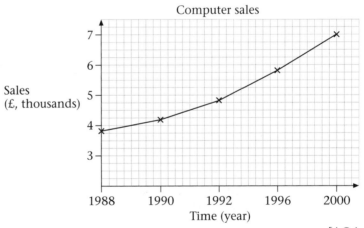

Computer sales

[AQA (SEG) 1999]

8 Scatter graphs

Scatter graphs are used to investigate a possible relationship between two sets of data. For example, you could use a scatter graph to investigate a possible link between people's height and their shoe size. By plotting the points on a scatter graph it is possible to show a link or **correlation** between the sets of data. To help analyse the points on a scatter graph a **line of best fit** is drawn. The line of best fit is the line that represents the distribution of the points best.

Drawing a line of best fit

In the exam, you will be asked to draw a line of best fit by eye. Using a ruler that is long enough to cover all the points on the graph, place it over the points and draw a straight line. The straight line should go through as many points as possible. Usually there will be points on either side of the line that you draw. When this happens, there should be about the same number of points on each side of the line.

Example 8.1

Draw a line of best fit on the following scatter graph.

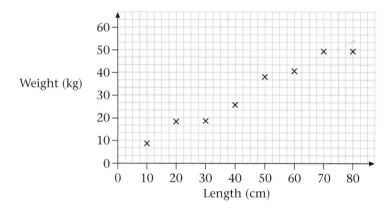

Solution

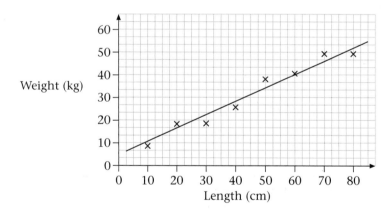

Interpreting scatter graphs

Once the line of best fit is drawn you will often be asked to comment on the correlation. The following graphs show the different types of correlation, you will have to remember these for the exam.

On the graph in Example 8.1, the scatter points are very close to a straight line that has a positive gradient. This data shows a **strong positive correlation**.

Reminder
A straight line with a positive gradient is one that goes uphill from left to right.

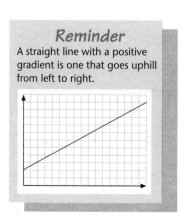

33

On the graph below, it is not possible to draw a single straight line through the points because they are widely scattered. In this case, we say there is little or **no correlation**.

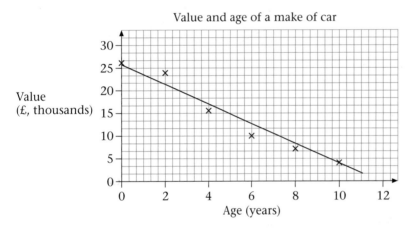

Marks in Maths and French exams

On this graph, the line of best fit has a negative gradient and the points are close to the line. This data shows a **strong negative correlation**.

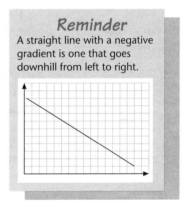

Reminder
A straight line with a negative gradient is one that goes downhill from left to right.

Value and age of a make of car

Example 8.2

The table shows the number of pages and the cost of eight children's books.

Number of pages	20	35	42	56	66	70	85	120
Cost (£)	2.50	2.90	3.00	2.70	3.50	3.90	4.20	5.00

a Plot the data as a scatter graph.

b Draw a line of best fit on your scatter graph.

c Describe the type of correlation shown in your graph.

d Use your line of best fit to estimate the cost of a children's book with 100 pages in it.

Solution

a When drawing a scatter graph the first variable given to you will be on the horizontal axis, so here the 'Number of pages' is along the horizontal axis. The second variable, 'Cost (£)', is on the vertical axis. Ensure you plot the points accurately.

b Draw a line that is as close as possible to all the points and has about the same number of points on either side of it. Your line must cover the whole range of the data. The line of best fit is shown above.

c The line of best fit has a positive gradient so the data shows a positive correlation. The points are fairly close to the line of best fit so you can say that the correlation is fairly strong.

d Go along the horizontal axis to 100 and draw in a vertical line to meet your line of best fit. Then draw a horizontal line across from that point to meet the vertical axis and read off that value carefully. An estimate of the cost of a children's book with 100 pages is about £4.50

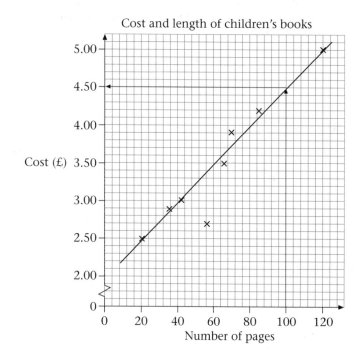

Cost and length of children's books

Practice questions

1 Eight people applied for a job. They each had an interview and a test. Their scores are shown in the table.

Person	A	B	C	D	E	F	G	H
Interview score	36	30	24	40	20	48	32	10
Test score	32	24	22	42	18	40	32	12

a Draw a scatter diagram for the data.

b What type of correlation is shown?

c Draw a line of best fit on your scatter diagram.

d Use your line of best fit to estimate the test score for another person whose interview score was 44.

> **Reminder**
> The first variable always goes on the horizontal axis.

[AQA (SEG) 2000]

2 The table shows the total number of unemployed adults and the total number of criminal offences committed for seven regions of England in 1993.

Region	Unemployed (thousands)	Offences (thousands)
North	170	35
Yorkshire and Humberside	240	69
East Midlands	180	44
East Anglia	80	12
South West	210	53
West Midlands	280	46
North West	320	80

(Please note these are not real figures.)

a Plot a scatter graph of this data.

b What type of correlation is shown?

c Draw a line of best fit on the scatter diagram.

d Use your line to estimate the total number of offences in a region with 130 thousand unemployed in 1993.

e In the South East, 920 thousand people were unemployed in 1993. Give one reason why it would *not* be sensible to extend your line on the scatter graph and use it to estimate the total number of offences for the South East.

EXAMINER *TIP*
Often axes are drawn for you. Make sure you read them carefully.

Reminder
Don't forget to put the units in your answer.

[AQA (SEG) 1997]

Practice exam questions

1 Eight GCSE students sat exams in Mathematics and Statistics. These are their marks.

Student	A	B	C	D	E	F	G	H
Mathematics	73	60	50	85	88	77	45	69
Statistics	78	66	52	85	95	80	49	72

a Plot a scatter graph of the data.

b What type of correlation is shown by these marks?

c Draw a line of best fit on the scatter diagram.

d Another student missed the Statistics exam but scored 80 marks in her Mathematics exam. Use your line of best fit to estimate a Statistics exam mark for this student.

EXAMINER *TIP*
Always use a ruler to draw the line of best fit and make sure it is long enough to cover the whole of the data.

[AQA (SEG) 1998]

2 Arnie takes his ice-cream van into the local park every Saturday. He thinks that his sales are affected by the maximum daytime temperature.

The table shows the maximum daytime temperature and Arnie's ice-cream sales for eight Saturdays.

Maximum daytime temperature (°C)	12	14	15	18	19	22	24	26
Sales (£)	75	90	120	150	200	175	210	250

a Use the information in the table to draw a scatter graph.

b Describe the relationship shown by the scatter graph.

c Draw a line of best fit on the scatter graph.

d Use your line of best fit to estimate Arnie's ice-cream sales in the park on a Saturday when the maximum temperature is 20 °C.

> EXAMINER **TIP**
> To describe the relationship it is not necessary to write out a full sentence. You can just state the type of correlation, e.g. positive correlation, negative correlation.

[AQA (SEG) 1999]

9 Cumulative frequency diagrams

Drawing a cumulative frequency graph

Cumulative means increasing as more of something is added. In a cumulative frequency table, the frequency of each class interval is added to the frequencies of the previous class intervals. The table below shows how the frequencies are cumulated.

> *Reminder*
> Class intervals are covered in Unit 2, Chapter 6 – Frequency diagrams.

Class intervals	Frequency	Cumulative frequency
$0 \leqslant x < 10$	3	3
$10 \leqslant x < 20$	8	11
$20 \leqslant x < 30$	15	26
$30 \leqslant x < 40$	4	30

> EXAMINER **TIP**
> Exam questions are often given as a grouped frequency table where the class intervals are of equal width.

A cumulative frequency graph can then be plotted. The cumulated frequencies are plotted against the upper class boundary of each class interval, e.g. in the class interval $10 \leqslant x < 20$, 20 is the upper class boundary. The upper class boundaries go on the horizontal axis with the cumulative frequency on the vertical axis. The cumulated frequencies increase as the upper class boundaries increase so the graph always has a positive gradient (although the line may not be straight).

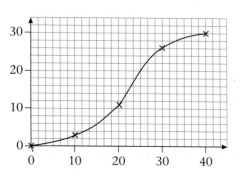

Example 9.1

The table shows the lifetimes (in hours) of a sample of 100 light bulbs.

Lifetime, *h* (hours)	Frequency
$750 \leqslant h < 850$	0
$850 \leqslant h < 950$	8
$950 \leqslant h < 1050$	54
$1050 \leqslant h < 1150$	32
$1150 \leqslant h < 1250$	6

EXAMINER *TIP*
These are the class intervals.

a Use the table above to draw a cumulative frequency table and draw a cumulative frequency diagram.

b Use your diagram to estimate the median.

Solution

a First draw a new table showing the upper class boundaries and the corresponding cumulative frequencies.

EXAMINER *TIP*
Remember that the frequency continually increases.

Lifetime, *h* (hours)	Cumulative frequency
< 850	0 (no bulbs less than 850)
< 950	8 (0 + 8 bulbs less than 950)
< 1050	62 (8 + 54 bulbs less than 1050)
< 1150	94 (62 + 32)
< 1250	100 (94 + 6)

EXAMINER *TIP*
Always check that the final cumulative frequency is the same as the total sample size.

You can think of a cumulative frequency diagram as a 'less than' diagram. This will help you to remember that you always have to plot the cumulative frequencies at the upper class boundaries, e.g. plot (850, 0), (950, 8), (1050, 62). Notice that the points continually increase.

Use the values in the table to plot the cumulative frequency diagram with Lifetime on the horizontal axis and the Cumulative frequency on the vertical axis.

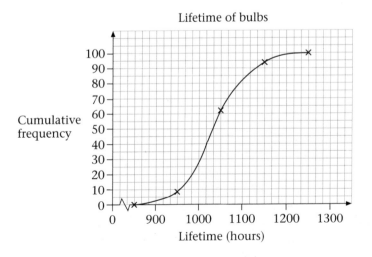

Lifetime of bulbs

Reminder
The cumulative frequency always goes on the vertical axis.

The points on the graph can be joined by a curve, as is shown above. If you are asked to draw a **cumulative frequency polygon**, you plot the Cumulative frequency against the upper class boundaries as usual. However, you join them using straight line segments as is shown on the graph below.

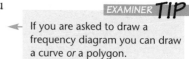

EXAMINER *TIP*

If you are asked to draw a frequency diagram you can draw a curve *or* a polygon.

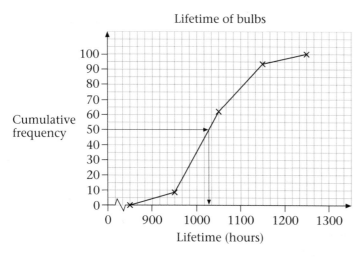

Lifetime of bulbs

b The median is the middle value in a set of data that has been arranged in order of size. It cuts a set of data exactly in two or, you could say, it is halfway through a large distribution. The frequency actually totals 100 in this example so 50% is the 50th value. Go up to 50 on the Cumulative frequency axis and draw a horizontal line to meet the curve. Then draw a vertical line down to meet the horizontal axis. Where your line cuts the horizontal axis is your estimate of the median. The median is about 1025 hours.

Reminder

You do not need to use the formula $\frac{n+1}{2}$ to find the middle value with continuous data. This is only used for discrete data.

Using a cumulative frequency curve

Interquartile range

Cumulative frequency curves help you to estimate the interquartile range.

Example 9.2

This cumulative frequency diagram shows the marks scored by 100 candidates in an exam. Use the diagram to calculate the interquartile range.

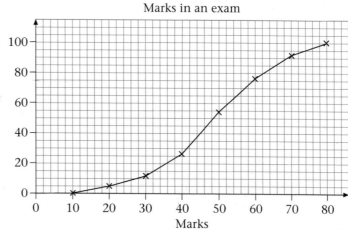

Marks in an exam

[AQA (SEG) 1999]

Solution

The interquartile range is a measure of spread of the middle 50% of the data. It is the difference between the upper quartile, Q_3 and the lower quartile, Q_1. Use the graph to estimate the values for Q_3 and Q_1.

The upper quartile (Q_3) is $\frac{3}{4}$ of the way through a large set of data, i.e. it is the 75th percentile.

$\frac{3}{4}$ of 100 = 75. From 75 on the Cumulative frequency axis, draw a horizontal line across to meet the curve. Then draw a vertical line down to meet the Marks axis. Where the line cuts the Marks axis is the Q_3 value. From this graph, the upper quartile is about 60 marks.

The lower quartile (Q_1) is $\frac{1}{4}$ of the way through a large set of data, i.e. it is the 25th percentile.

$\frac{1}{4}$ of 100 = 25. From 25 on the cumulative frequency axis, draw a horizontal line across to meet the curve. Then draw a vertical line down to meet the Marks axis. From this graph, the lower quartile is about 40 marks.

> **Reminder**
> You do not need to use the formulae $\frac{n+1}{4}$ or $\frac{3(n+1)}{4}$ to find the quartiles. They are only used for discrete data.

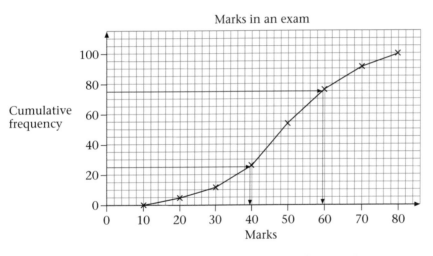

Marks in an exam

> *EXAMINER* **TIP**
> When reading from the graph, always draw in the working lines to show your method.

The interquartile range is $Q_3 - Q_1 = 60 - 40 = 20$ marks

In this example, although the range of the marks was 70, the interquartile range was about 20. This suggests that the marks were clustered around the middle of the distribution. The smaller the interquartile range the more clustered the data is.

Estimating frequencies

Often a question is given to test that you can use or interpret a cumulative frequency curve.

Example 9.3

Using the graph in Example 9.2 find how many candidates scored:

a less than 40 marks

b 70 marks or more.

Solution

a Draw a vertical line from 40 on the Marks axis up to the curve. Then draw a horizontal line across to the Cumulative frequency axis. Where the line cuts the vertical axis shows the number of students who scored less than 40 marks. On the graph below 26 candidates scored less than 40 marks.

b Draw a vertical line up from 70 on the Marks axis. Then draw a horizontal line across to the Cumulative frequency axis. On the graph shown about 92 students scored less than 70 marks. To find how many students scored 70 marks or more take this value away from the total number of students. 100 – 92 = 8. 8 students scored 70 marks or more.

> **Reminder**
> The curve on a cumulative frequency diagram is a less than curve.

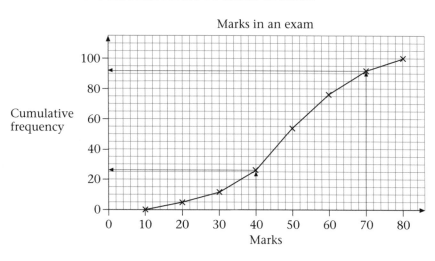

Marks in an exam

Practice questions

1 A company employs 80 sales people who use their own cars to visit customers. Their annual business mileages are listed in the table below.

Annual business mileage	Number of sales people
0 to less than 10 000	6
10 000 to less than 20 000	14
20 000 to less than 30 000	26
30 000 to less than 40 000	19
40 000 to less than 50 000	7
50 000 to less than 60 000	5
60 000 to less than 70 000	3

   a Draw and complete a suitable cumulative frequency table for this data.

   b Draw a cumulative frequency curve for this data.

   c Use your graph to estimate the median mileage.

   d Use your graph to find the interquartile range of the mileages.

The company increased the mileage payments for all sales people who travelled more than 45 000 miles in one year.

  e Use your graph to estimate how many of the sales people got this increased payment.

2 The table shows the amount of time students spend watching television per week.

Hours per week	Number of students	Cumulative frequency
0 to less than 15	0	
15 to less than 20	2	
20 to less than 25	8	
25 to less than 30	13	
30 to less than 35	15	
35 to less than 40	12	
40 to less than 45	6	
45 to less than 50	4	

  a Copy the table and complete the cumulative frequency column.

  b Draw a cumulative frequency curve.

  c Use your graph to obtain:

    i   the median

    ii   the interquartile range

    iii   the number of students who watched television for more than 43 hours per week.

                                             [AQA (SEG) 1997]

Practice exam question

1 The table shows the lengths of time for which cars were parked in a car park.

Time, t (hours)	Number of cars	Cumulative frequency
$0 \leqslant t < 1$	15	
$1 \leqslant t < 2$	25	
$2 \leqslant t < 4$	30	
$4 \leqslant t < 6$	10	
$6 \leqslant t < 9$	8	
$9 \leqslant t < 12$	2	

  a Copy the table and complete the cumulative frequency column. Use the table to draw a cumulative frequency curve.

  b Use your graph to estimate the number of cars that were parked for more than five hours.

                                             [AQA (SEG) 1998]

10 Box plots

Box plots are used frequently to represent sets, or distributions, of data. They are also commonly known as box-and-whisker diagrams.

A box plot indicates *five important points* in a distribution. They look like this.

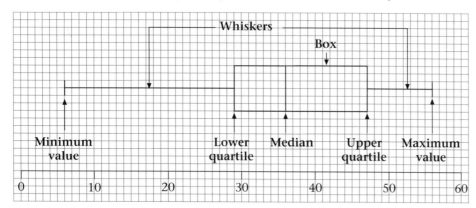

The box represents the middle 50% of the distribution and the whiskers show the spread of the distribution.

Box plots can be plotted horizontally side by side so that you can quickly compare two or more distributions.

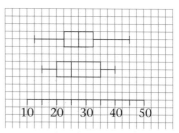

Example 10.1

The numbers of cars entering a tunnel were measured over 10 minute periods. These were the results.

12   15   18   10   17   22   35   11   14   21   28

Draw a box plot for this data.

Solution

Firstly you need to locate the five important points for this data. To do this you will need to order the data.

10   11   12   14   15   17   18   21   22   28   35

The highest and lowest values can be seen once the data is ordered.

Highest value = 35   Lowest value = 10

Find the median first, then the upper and lower quartiles next.

You find the median by using the formula to find its position.

Position of median is $\dfrac{(n+1)}{2} = \dfrac{(11+1)}{2} = 6$

Count along to the position of the median (the sixth value in this example).

Median = 17

Find the positions of the lower and upper quartiles by using the formulas.

Lower quartile position $= \dfrac{(n+1)}{4} = \dfrac{(11+1)}{4} = 3$

Upper quartile position $= \dfrac{3(n+1)}{4} = \dfrac{3(11+1)}{4} = 9$

Count along the ordered set of data to the third and ninth values.

Lower quartile = 12   Upper quartile = 22

Once you have located the five important points plot them on your graph paper and complete the diagram by drawing the box and the whiskers.

The height of the box does not matter but if you are drawing two or more box plots side by side then the heights of the boxes should be equal.

Number of cars entering a tunnel

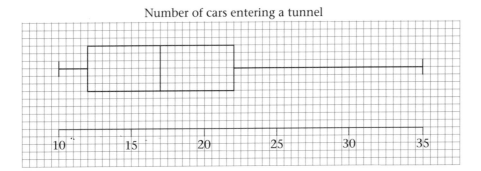

Comparing box plots

In the exam, you may be asked to compare two box plots. When comparing box plots you should include a comparison of spread (range, interquartile range) and a comparison of average (median) between the two distributions.

Example 10.2

a Use the data in the table to draw the two box plots on the same axes.

b Write down two comparisons between the two box plots.

Data	Minimum	Lower Quartile	Median	Upper Quartile	Maximum
A	12	20	25	30	38
B	9	18	22	28	42

Solution

a

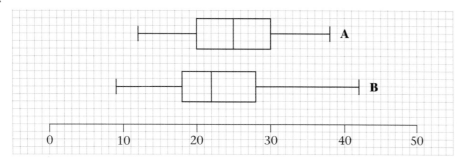

b The two comparisons should be about average and spread.

It is clear that distribution B has a wider range (42 – 9 = 33) than distribution A (38 – 12 = 26). The distribution A has a larger median than distribution B (25 > 22).

EXAMINER *TIP*

When comparing box plots it is better to give your answers in the context of the question if possible. Here, there is no context so none is included in the answer.

Practice questions

1 Draw the following two box plots on the same axes. Write down two comparisons between the two box plots.

Data	Minimum	Lower Quartile	Median	Upper Quartile	Maximum
P	14	26	32	42	54
Q	8	24	35	38	46

2 The lengths (in mm) of 20 leaves were measured and recorded as follows.

45   25   25   28   34   16   18   25   33   38

44   32   18   26   27   42   40   38   33   21

Use the data to:

a work out the five important points that are needed to draw a box plot

b draw a box plot of the data

c calculate the range and the interquartile range of the data.

3 Carry out a quick survey, or invent your own data, for one of the following:

● the number of cars parked in your street each evening at 5 pm, 6 pm and 7 pm for a week

● the number of pupils in each class in your school at a certain time on one day

● the amount of money that each of 20 of your friends spent on their mobile phone last month.

Draw a box plot of the data and write down two comments about the distribution.

Practice exam question

1 The weights of 80 bags of rice are measured. The table summarises the results.

Minimum	480 g
Lower quartile	500 g
Median	540 g
Upper quartile	620 g
Maximum	720 g

a Copy the axis and draw a box plot to show this information.

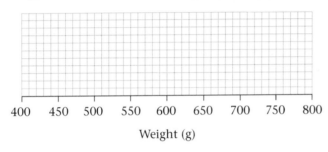

Weight (g)

b Write down the interquartile range for the data.

c How many bags weigh:

   i   less than 480 g?

   ii less than 500 g?

[AQA 2002]

11 Moving averages

Moving averages is a method of smoothing out changes in data over a period of time. It can be used to show trends in data.

Each moving average value is the mean of consecutive groups of values throughout the data.

EXAMINER **TIP**

Moving averages is really a calculator topic and so would almost always appear in the calculator section of the exam.

Types of moving average

The number of values grouped together depends upon the seasonality of the data, e.g. if the data was collected over five days in a week you would need to calculate a 5 point moving average. The table highlights the appropriate moving average for different time series data.

Time series data	Appropriate moving average
Quarterly data (4 quarters)	4 point
Termly data (3 terms)	3 point
Semester (half-yearly)	2 point
7 day week	7 point
5 day week	5 point
Car sales (monthly)	12 point or 6 point

Practice question 1

1 Copy and complete the table below.

Time series data	Appropriate moving average
Gas bills (quarterly)	
Cinema attendances (daily)	
Student enrollment (3 terms)	
Mobile phone bills (monthly)	
Shop sales (5 days per week)	
Council rates (twice yearly)	

EXAMINER **TIP**

You will probably not get a question involving more than a 6 point moving average.

Calculating and plotting moving averages

You will often be asked to plot the data as a time series graph and then plot the moving averages on the same graph. To calculate moving averages you first decide which point size to use, then group the values together according to that point size. If you were using a 4 point average you would find the mean of the first, second, third and fourth values and then the mean of the second, third, fourth and fifth values, etc. until all the values have been included and then plot the averages against the midpoints.

Example 11.1

The following sales (in £) were recorded by a market trader over four days for three weeks. Calculate the moving averages and then plot them on a graph.

Sales week	Day	Sales (£)
1	Monday	250
	Tuesday	280
	Friday	640
	Saturday	750
2	Monday	290
	Tuesday	300
	Friday	680
	Saturday	830
3	Monday	270
	Tuesday	260
	Friday	640
	Saturday	790

Solution

There are four data points in each week that the data is recorded over so it is necessary to calculate a 4 point moving average. The first 4 point moving average is the mean of the first four data values.

$$\frac{250 + 280 + 640 + 750}{4} = 480$$

This value (480) has to be plotted on the time series graph at the horizontal time period that is exactly halfway between the four data values used to calculate this average, i.e. halfway between Tuesday and Friday in week one.

The second 4 point moving average is then the average of the second, third, fourth and fifth data values:

$$\frac{280 + 640 + 750 + 290}{4} = 490$$

This value (490) has to be plotted on the time axis at the mid-point of the 4 data values used to calculate this average i.e. halfway between Friday and Saturday in week one.

For the third 4 point moving average the third, fourth, fifth and sixth values are used. This process continues throughout the whole of the data to give nine different 4 point moving averages.

Sales Week	Day	Sales (£)	4 point moving average
1	Monday	250	
	Tuesday	280	
	Friday	640	480
	Saturday	750	490
2	Monday	290	495
	Tuesday	300	505
	Friday	680	525
	Saturday	830	520
3	Monday	270	510
	Tuesday	260	500
	F		490
	S		

Once you have calc   ne series
graph and then plot   es are
each plotted at the   calculate
each moving avera   lated from
an even number o   e value
will not align verti   verages
can be joined by st   )est fit.
Here they are join

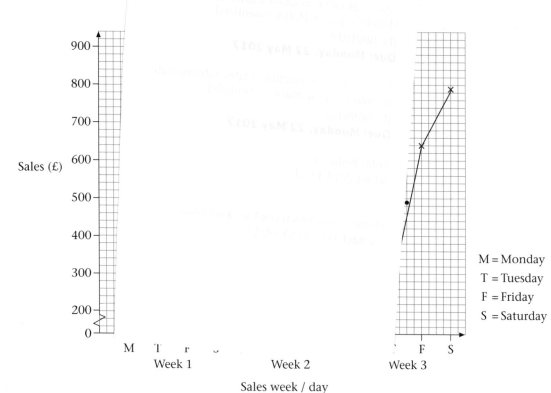

M = Monday
T = Tuesday
F = Friday
S = Saturday

Sales (£)

Sales week / day

Week 1   Week 2   Week 3

Example 11.2

The student enrollment at a Law department each semester (every six months) at an American university is shown in the table together with the 2 point moving averages.

Use the table to plot a time series graph and then plot the moving averages.

Year	Semester	Enrollment	2 point moving average
2000	Spring	220	
			200
	Fall	180	
			205
2001	Spring	230	
			215
	Fall	200	
			225
2002	Spring	250	
			240
	Fall	230	

Solution

Draw the data as a time series graph. Then use the fourth column in the table to plot the moving averages. On this graph, the points are joined using a line of best fit.

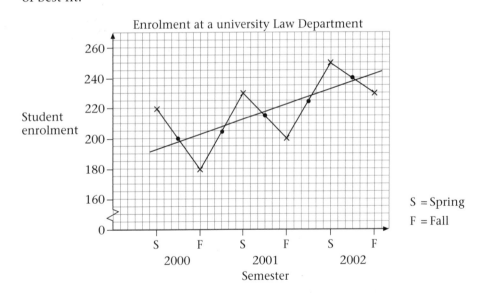

EXAMINER **TIP**

← The moving averages are plotted halfway between the data values used to calculate the moving average, so the first 2 point moving average is halfway between the first two data values.

S = Spring
F = Fall

Example 11.3

A youth club is open on Sundays, Wednesdays and Fridays. The table shows the attendances at the youth club over a month.

Day	Attendance
Sunday	54
Wednesday	35
Friday	60
Sunday	61
Wednesday	38
Friday	66
Sunday	72
Wednesday	43
Friday	64
Sunday	68
Wednesday	45
Friday	68
Sunday	71

a   Which moving average is appropriate for this data?

b   Calculate the moving averages and plot them with the original data on a time series graph.

Solution

a   A 3 point moving average is appropriate for this data because the data is for three days every week.

b   Since there are a lot of calculations to perform it is useful to add two extra columns to the table to calculate the 3 point moving totals and the 3 point moving averages.

The first 3 point moving total is the total of the first three values, i.e. 54 + 35 + 60 = 149. This total is written in the appropriate position in the table halfway between the three data values opposite 35.

The moving totals are then listed for all the remaining data values. You then divide all the moving totals by three to give the 3 point moving averages.

Day	Attendance	3 point moving total	3 point moving average
Sunday	54		
Wednesday	35	149	49.7
Friday	60	156	52.0
Sunday	61	159	53.0
Wednesday	38	165	55.0
Friday	66	176	58.7
Sunday	72	181	60.3
Wednesday	43	179	59.7
Friday	64	175	58.3
Sunday	68	177	59.0
Wednesday	45	181	60.3
Friday	68	184	61.3
Sunday	71		

The moving averages should then be plotted at the mid-point of each three day period, i.e. aligned with an actual data value.

EXAMINER **TIP**

When plotting the time series graph, make sure the data is plotted over three days for each week not seven days. This is because the data is not spread over seven days as the Youth club is only open on Sundays, Wednesdays and Fridays.

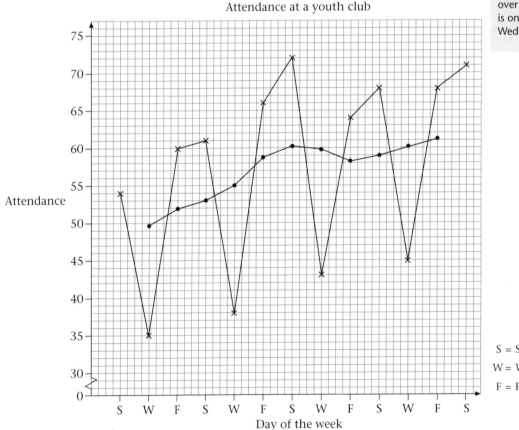

Attendance at a youth club

Attendance

Day of the week

S = Sunday

W = Wednesday

F = Friday

Drawing a trend line

In Example 11.3, the straight lines joining consecutive moving average values show a slight upward trend. If you were to use the trend to forecast into the future, it would be appropriate to use a single straight trend line like a line of best fit through the moving average values.

The trend line is usually a line of best fit through the moving average points.

Example 11.4

Use the graph drawn in Example 11.3 on page 52 to:

a insert a trend line

b comment on the attendance at this youth club.

Solution

a The trend line shown is appropriate. It is joined by straight line segments. If you were planning to use the trend line to predict values in the future, a line of best fit would be more appropriate.

b The trend line shows a slight increase suggesting that the attendance at the youth club is slightly increasing from week to week. You could also comment upon the fluctuation of the attendances over the days; it appears that Fridays and Sundays are more popular than Wednesdays.

Using the trend to predict future values

Two common methods of forecasting values into the future using the line of best fit are the **reverse average method** and the **seasonal component method**.

Reverse average method

Consider the data and graph in Example 11.2.

Year	Semester	Enrolment	2 point moving average
2000	Spring	220	
	Fall	180	200
2001	Spring	230	205
	Fall	200	215
2002	Spring	250	225
	Fall	226	238

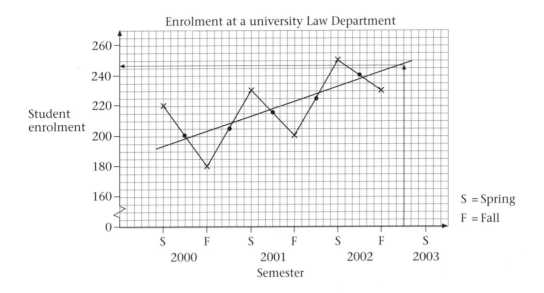

The line of best fit has been extended to where the moving average for Fall 2002 and Spring 2003 would be.

Use the extended trend line to estimate the next moving average value on the time series graph. This can be called the trend value, t. In this example, t is 246.

Then use the value t to calculate the unknown forecast value, x (value for Spring 2003).

$$t \text{ is } \frac{(226 + x)}{2} = 246$$
$$226 + x = 2 \times 246$$
$$226 + x = 492$$
$$x = 492 - 226$$
$$x = 266$$

Therefore, the forecast for the number of students enrolling for Law in the Spring of 2003 is 264.

Example 11.5

Consider the data for the attendances at the youth club in Example 11.3 on pages 51 and 52. Use the graph to forecast the attendance for the following Wednesday.

Solution

First draw a line of best fit about the moving average points and extend it to past the last Sunday.

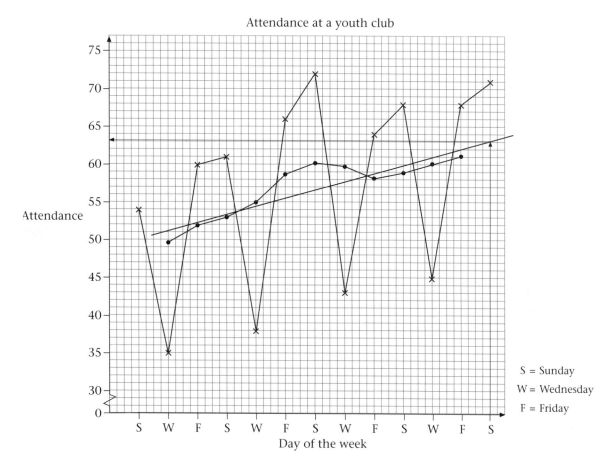

Read off the next estimated moving average value (the one that coincides with the last Sunday) and call this the first trend value, t_1. This value is 63. Use the value for t_1 to find x_1, the forecasted value for Wednesday.

$$t_1 \text{ is } \frac{(68 + 71 + x_1)}{3} = 63$$

$$68 + 71 + x_1 = 3 \times 63$$

$$68 + 71 + x_1 = 189$$

$$x_1 = 189 - 68 - 71$$

$$x_1 = 50$$

Therefore, the forecast of attendance at the youth club on the following Wednesday is 50.

Seasonal component method

This method involves finding a seasonal component and adding it to the estimated trend value at the period you are forecasting.

Example 11.6

The quarterly energy bills for a small firm are recorded in the table below.

Quarter-Year	Energy bills (£)
Q1–2001	200
Q2–2001	80
Q3–2001	65
Q4–2001	235
Q1–2002	215
Q2–2002	100
Q3–2002	70
Q4–2002	250

a Calculate the appropriate moving averages for this data.

b Plot the actual data and the moving averages onto graph paper.

c Use the trend line to estimate the Q1 energy bill for 2003.

Solution

a Calculate the 4 point moving averages because the given data is quarterly (four quarters per year).

Quarter-Year	Energy bills (£)	4 point moving average
Q1–2001	200	
Q2–2001	80	
		145.00
Q3–2001	65	
		148.75
Q4–2001	235	
		153.75
Q1–2002	215	
		155.00
Q2–2002	100	
		158.75
Q3–2002	70	
Q4–2002	250	

b Plot the data as a time series graph first. Then plot the moving averages in their correct positions, i.e. the first 4 point moving average (145) must be exactly halfway between the Q2 and Q3 figures for 2001.

c Draw in the trend line as a straight line passing through the moving average plots (like a line of best fit). Use the graph to find the seasonal component for Q1. Draw in vertical lines joining the data plotted at each Q1 value with the trend line and measure the differences between the data and the trend. The Q1 values are 65 and 55 above the trend line. The average seasonal component for Q1 is the mean of these values.

Q1 average seasonal component is $\dfrac{65 + 60}{2} = 62.5$

Use the trend line to estimate the trend for Q1 in 2003 – it appears to be £180. Since the average seasonal component for Q1 is above the trend then we can estimate the energy bill for Q1 in 2003 by adding the seasonal component to the estimated trend value.

Q1 2003 energy bill is £180 + £62.5 = £242.5

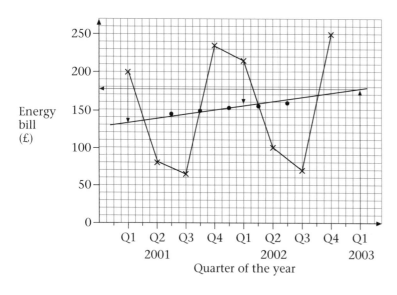

Practice questions 2

1 a Calculate the 3 point moving averages for the following data.

Jimmy's absences from school

Year 9			Year 10			Year 11		
Autumn term	Spring term	Summer term	Autumn term	Spring term	Summer term	Autumn term	Spring term	Summer term
20	12	14	24	14	18	30	16	21

b Plot the data as a time series graph.

c Plot the moving averages onto your graph and draw in a trend line.

d Comment upon Jimmy's absences from school.

2 The quarterly telephone charges (in £) for Tracy over the past two years are shown in the table.

	2001				2002			
Quarter	Q1	Q2	Q3	Q4	Q1	Q2	Q3	Q4
Charge (£)	50	55	61	62	58	64	69	75

a Plot the data as a time series graph.

b Which moving average is appropriate for this data?

c Calculate all the moving averages and plot them in their appropriate positions on the time series graph.

d Draw in a trend line.

e Use the trend line to forecast Tracy's telephone charge for Q1 2003.

Practice exam question

1 A college records the number of people who sign up for adult education classes each term. The table shows the numbers from Autumn 2000 to Summer 2002.

Term	Autumn 2000	Spring 2001	Summer 2001	Autumn 2001	Spring 2002	Summer 2002
Number of people	520	300	380	640	540	500

a Calculate the first value of the 3 point moving average for the data.

b Explain why a 3 point moving average is appropriate.

c Plot the raw data as a time series graph.

d Calculate all the other 3 point moving averages and plot all the moving averages on a graph in their correct positions.

e Draw in a trend line and use it to estimate the 3 point moving average that would be plotted at Summer 2002.

f Use the value obtained in part e to calculate a prediction of the number of people who will sign up for adult education classes in Autumn 2002.

[AQA 2002]

12 Mean of a discrete frequency distribution

The most common measure of an average is the arithmetic mean, $\bar{x}$ (pronounced x-bar). The mean of a set of data is calculated by summing all the values and then dividing by the number of values.

$$\bar{x} = \frac{\text{Sum of all the values}}{\text{Total frequency}}$$

This can be written using the appropriate mathematical symbols.

$\bar{x} = \dfrac{\sum x}{n}$ where $\bar{x}$ is the arithmetic mean, the $\sum$ (Greek capital letter sigma) is the sum of all of the values, x represents the individual values and n is the number of values.

Example 12.1

Find the mean of the following ten values.

9   12   13   6   19   15   6   9   11   15

Solution

There are 10 values so $n = 10$.

$\sum x = 9 + 12 + 13 + 6 + 19 + 15 + 6 + 9 + 11 + 15$

$\quad = 115$

Use the formula to find the arithmetic mean:

$\bar{x}$ is $\dfrac{\sum x}{n} = \dfrac{115}{10} = 11.5$

Frequency distributions

A frequency distribution, or frequency table, is a way of recording large sets of data. A frequency table shows the frequency associated with each discrete value or with each class interval.

In Example 12.1, there are ten values. We could have recorded them in a discrete frequency table as follows.

Value, x	Frequency, f
6	2
9	2
11	1
12	1
13	1
15	2
19	1

To calculate the mean of this distribution you need to sum all the values and divide this total by the number of values.

The total frequency is the number of values n. In this example $n = 10$ because there are ten values altogether. The total frequency can also be represented by the symbols $\sum f$.

The table shows the frequency of each value, e.g. there are two sixes, two nines, etc. To sum all the values in one go would be difficult. So an extra column is often provided for you to calculate the frequency, f, multiplied by the value, x, for each row of the table.

Value, x	Frequency, f	$f \times x$
6	2	12
9	2	18
11	1	11
12	1	12
13	1	13
15	2	30
19	1	19
Total	$n = 10$	$\sum fx = 115$

EXAMINER TIP

If an extra column isn't provided, draw your own. Tables are usually shown on the left-hand side to give you room to add an extra column.

Reminder
The total frequency is the number of values, n.

After completing all the rows in the $f \times x$ column you need to add up all of those products to get $\sum fx$ (which is the total of all the values in this distribution).

$$\sum fx = 12 + 18 + 11 + 12 + 13 + 30 + 19$$

$$= 115$$

Use the formula to find the arithmetic mean:

$$\bar{x} \text{ is } \frac{\sum fx}{n} = \frac{115}{10} = 11.5$$

You may think that this is a rather complicated way of finding the mean of a simple set of data but when the number of values is large (>30) this method is easier than trying to add all the values individually.

The arithmetic mean will rarely be a whole number. You should not round your answer to a whole number even when a decimal number does not make sense. For example, on average there are 2.4 children per family, though clearly there is no such thing as 0.4 of a child.

Example 12.2

The owner of a small electrical shop carried out a survey of 50 local families. One of the questions on the survey was about the number of television sets that each family owned. The results of this question are shown in the table.

Number of televisions owned	Number of families	
0	0	
1	5	
2	20	
3	17	
4	6	
5	2	

Copy the table and use the blank column to calculate the mean number of televisions per family.

[AQA (SEG) 1997]

Solution

You are told in the question that the total number of families is 50; this is the value of n. Always check this with the table values that are given to you, i.e. check $\sum f = 50$.

In this example, the numbers of televisions owned are the x values and the numbers of families are the frequencies, f. The blank column in the table is for you to complete the $f \times x$ values for each row. Then sum these to get $\sum fx$, the total sum of all the values.

> **Reminder**
> You can use n or $\sum f$ for the total frequency.

Number of televisions owned, x	Number of families, f	$f \times x$
0	0	0
1	5	5
2	20	40
3	17	51
4	6	24
5	2	10
Total	$\sum f = 50$	$\sum fx = 130$

Use the values of $\sum f$ and $\sum fx$ to calculate $\bar{x}$.

$$\bar{x} \text{ is } \frac{\sum fx}{\sum f} = \frac{130}{50} = 2.6$$

You should use always check that your answer is sensible for the given data. In this case there were approximately 130 TV's in total and 50 families. So $\bar{x}$ would be approximately 150 divided by 50, which equals 3. The calculated value (2.6) is close to this approximation and therefore is sensible for the given data.

Practice questions

1 The table shows the number of fish caught by anglers in one day. Calculate the mean number of fish caught by these anglers.

Number of fish caught	Number of anglers
0	3
1	12
2	10
3	8
4	5
5	2

2 The table shows the number of pupils in each class at a school. Calculate the mean number of pupils per class.

Number of pupils in a class	Number of classes
20	6
23	4
24	5
25	10
27	8
29	2

Practice exam question

1 Jan carried out a survey of 900 houses in a village. She found out how many people were living at each house. Her results are shown in the table.

Number of people	Number of houses
1	73
2	142
3	195
4	380
5	110

Calculate the mean number of people per house.   [AQA (SEG) 2000]

13 Grouped data

Mean of grouped data

With large sets of data (or large distributions of data) it is often necessary to group the data into class intervals so that it can be represented in a form that is easier to understand.

Data that is continuous (e.g. heights, lengths, masses, weights) will always have to be grouped into class intervals because very few values will be identical to each other. It seems sensible for data to have equal class widths. However, this is not always the case especially if there are very large or very small values that are untypical of the rest of the distribution, e.g. a set of students' exam results where one student was ill for most of the year and did very little in the exam.

> **Reminder**
> The class boundaries must not overlap.

Once the original raw data has been summarised into a grouped frequency table you can no longer know the individual data values. This means it is not possible to calculate the exact mean of this data when it is given in this form.

We can only calculate an estimate of the mean by using the mid-points of the class intervals as the x values. Often an extra one or two columns will be given to you on the right-hand side of the grouped frequency table to help you calculate an estimate of the mean. Calculate the mid-point of each class interval. Then find the value $f \times x$ for each class interval by multiplying the mid-point by the frequency.

> **EXAMINER TIP**
> If the extra columns are not given, draw them in.

Class interval	Frequency, f	Mid-point, x	$f \times x$
1–5	0	3	0
6–10	4	8	32
11–15	5	13	65
16–20	1	18	18
Total	$n = 10$		$\sum fx = 115$

> **Reminder**
> You find the mid-point by adding the upper and lower class boundaries and dividing by 2.

> **Reminder**
> You can use n or $\sum f$ to mean the total frequency.

Use the formula to estimate the value for $\bar{x}$. $\bar{x}$ is $\dfrac{\sum fx}{n} = \dfrac{115}{10} = 11.5$

Example 13.1

The weights of 50 frozen turkeys are shown in the table.

a Write down the mid-point of the class interval 3 kg to less than 4 kg.

b Calculate an estimate of the mean weight of the frozen turkeys.

Weight (kg)	Frequency
3 to less than 4	9
4 to less than 5	11
5 to less than 6	10
6 to less than 7	14
7 to less than 8	6

[AQA (SEG) 1998]

Solution

a This data is continuous data. The class interval 3 kg to less than 4 kg has a mid-point halfway between 3 and 4. So the mid-point is 3.5.

b This question has not given you the two extra blank columns on the right-hand side of the table. So you can insert them yourself or use the working lines in the questions as if they were rows.

Weight (kg)	Frequency, f	Mid-point, x	$f \times x$
3 to less than 4	9	3.5	31.5
4 to less than 5	11	4.5	49.5
5 to less than 6	10	5.5	55.0
6 to less than 7	14	6.5	91.0
7 to less than 8	6	7.5	45.0
Total	$\sum f = 50$		$\sum fx = 272$

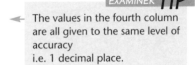

The values in the fourth column are all given to the same level of accuracy i.e. 1 decimal place.

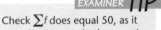

Check $\sum f$ does equal 50, as it was given to you in the question.

Reminder
Check that the estimate of the mean seems reasonable.

$$\bar{x} \text{ is } \frac{\sum fx}{\sum f} = \frac{272}{50} = 5.44 \text{ kg}$$

Practice questions 1

1 For his Statistics project Rashid carried out an investigation into the lengths of words in a local newspaper. The frequency table shows the lengths of 300 words, selected at random, from the local newspaper.

Length of word	Frequency, f		
1–3	110		
4–6	130		
7–9	45		
10–12	10		
13–15	5		

Calculate an estimate of the mean length of a word from the local newspaper.

[AQA (SEG) 1999]

2 John organised a paper plane competition for a group of scouts. The distances (in metres) flown by each plane were recorded.

Distance, x (m)	Number of planes
$0.0 < x \leq 10.0$	24
$10.0 < x \leq 20.0$	14
$20.0 < x \leq 30.0$	8
$30.0 < x \leq 40.0$	3
$40.0 < x \leq 50.0$	1

Calculate an estimate of the mean distance flown.

Modal class for grouped data

The **mode** is the most common value in a set of data. When data has been grouped into class intervals of equal width the **modal class** is the class with the highest frequency.

You may be asked to write down the modal class from a set of data. It could be given in the form of a grouped frequency table or from a histogram drawn with class intervals of equal width.

Example 13.2

Use the table to write down the modal class for the data.

Class interval	Frequency, f
6–10	14
11–15	18
16–20	8

Solution

You can see that the class intervals are all of equal width; 6–10, 11–15 and 16–20 are all of width 5 units. Therefore the class interval with highest frequency will be the modal class. The class interval with the highest frequency is 11–15. So this data has a modal class of 11–15.

Example 13.3

Use the histogram to write down the modal class for the data.

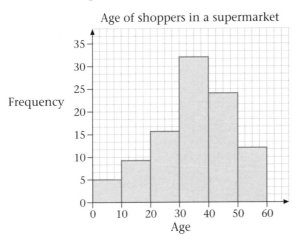

Age of shoppers in a supermarket

Solution

The histogram has equal class widths and therefore you select the class interval that has the greatest height.

The class interval with the greatest height is 30–39. So the modal class from this diagram is 30–39.

> *Reminder*
> Histograms are covered in Unit 2, Chapter 6, Frequency diagrams

Practice questions 2

1 Write down the modal class of each of the following grouped frequency tables.

a

Weight (kg)	Frequency
3 to less than 4	9
4 to less than 5	13
5 to less than 6	15
6 to less than 7	18
7 to less than 8	3

[AQA (SEG) 1998]

b

Length of word	Frequency
1–3 letters	135
4–6 letters	150
7–9 letters	85
10–12 letters	10
13–15 letters	5

c

Distance, x (metres)	Frequency
$0.0 < x \leqslant 10.0$	24
$10.0 < x \leqslant 20.0$	14
$20.0 < x \leqslant 30.0$	8
$30.0 < x \leqslant 40.0$	3
$40.0 < x \leqslant 50.0$	1

2 Write down the modal class of each of the following histograms.

a

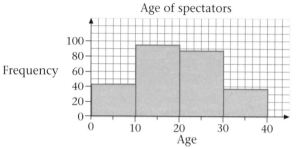

b

c

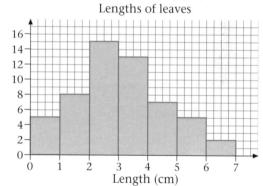

Finding the median from a table

The median of a set of data is the value that is positioned exactly halfway through the data (when the data is arranged in order of size).

When data is shown in discrete and grouped frequency tables it is necessary to identify where the median position is within the table.

You can use the formula $\frac{(n+1)}{2}$ to find the position of the median.

Finding the median from a discrete frequency distribution

Example 13.4

Use the table to find the median of the set of data.

Value, x	Frequency, f	
6	2	
8	2	
10	1	
12	1	
14	1	
15	2	
18	1	
20	2	

Solution

With such a small set of data you would normally arrange the data in order of size and locate the $\dfrac{(n+1)}{2}$ item, i.e. the 6.5th value. However when this data is given as a discrete frequency distribution you have to locate where the median must lie. Adding up the frequencies you find there are 12 values in the set of data. The position of median is the 6.5th value. Use the blank column on the right-hand side of the table to cumulate the frequencies until you find the 6.5th value. The sixth value is 12 and the seventh value is 14 so the 6.5th value is 13. The median of this data set is 13.

Value, x	Frequency, f	CF
6	2	2
8	2	4
10	1	5
12	1	6
14	1	7
15	2	9
18	1	10
20	2	12

CF = Cumulative frequency

Practice questions 3

1 Find the median for each of the following discrete frequency distributions.

a

Class size	Number of classes
15	8
16	7
17	24
18	25
19	12
20	9

b

Number of children	Number of families
0	8
1	46
2	22
3	17
4	3

Finding the class interval that contains the median

When the data is given as a grouped frequency table you can no longer find the exact median of the data. This is because you do not know what the individual data values are. You can, however, find the class interval that contains the median.

The table shows the data from Example 13.4 put into class intervals.

Class interval	Frequency, f	Cumulative frequency
6–10	5	5
11–15	4	9
16–20	3	12
Total	$\Sigma f = 12$	

There are 12 data values altogether. This can be used to calculate the position of the median.

Position of the median is $\dfrac{(n+1)}{2} = 6.5$

The position of the median is the 6.5th value. Use a blank column on the right-hand side of the table to cumulate the frequencies until you find the 6.5th value.

There are five values in the first class interval, since there are another four values in the second class interval then there are nine values in the first two class intervals. Therefore, the sixth value, the seventh value, the eighth value and the ninth value all lie in the second class interval 11–15. You know that the median is the value in the 6.5th position and so the median must lie in the second class interval.

The class interval that contains the median is 11–15.

Example 13.5

Find the class interval that contains the median for the following large set of data.

Class interval	Frequency, f	
1–3	90	
4–6	130	
7–9	145	
10–12	70	
13–15	45	
16–18	22	
19–21	8	
Total	$\Sigma f = 510$	

Solution

Firstly sum up the frequencies to find out how many values there are in this distribution. You can write the total frequency at the bottom of the frequency column. There are 510 data values.

Secondly use the formula to locate the median position.

Position of the median is $\dfrac{(n+1)}{2} = \dfrac{(510+1)}{2} = 255.5$

Thirdly cumulate the frequencies and put them in the third column until you find where the 255.5th value lies. There are 220 values in the first two class intervals and there are 365 values in the first three class intervals. Since the median is the 255.5th value it must lie in the third class interval. The class interval that contains the median is 7–9.

Class interval	Frequency, f	CF
1–3	90	90
4–6	130	220
7–9	145	365
10–12	70	435
13–15	45	480
16–18	22	502
19–21	8	510
Total	$\Sigma f = 510$	

EXAMINER *TIP*

Do not be fooled into thinking that the middle class interval is the class interval that contains the median.

Practice questions 4

1 Find the class interval that contains the median for each of the following sets of data.

a

Weight (kg)	Frequency, f
3 to less than 4	9
4 to less than 5	11
5 to less than 6	10
6 to less than 7	14
7 to less than 8	6

b

Distance, x (metres)	Number of planes
$0.0 < x \leqslant 10.0$	24
$10.0 < x \leqslant 20.0$	14
$20.0 < x \leqslant 30.0$	8
$30.0 < x \leqslant 40.0$	3
$40.0 < x \leqslant 50.0$	1

c

Time, t (seconds)	Number of boys
$12.0 < t \leqslant 13.0$	5
$13.0 < t \leqslant 14.0$	15
$14.0 < t \leqslant 15.0$	18
$15.0 < t \leqslant 16.0$	12

2 The numbers of words in the first 100 sentences of a novel are shown in the table.

Number of words	Frequency
1–9	18
10–19	34
20–29	43
30–39	4
40–49	1

Write down the class interval that contains the median.

Practice exam questions

1 Jack records how long it takes 50 boys to run the 100 metres. His results are shown in the table. Calculate an estimate of the mean time.

Time, t (seconds)	Number of boys		
$12.0 < t \leq 13.0$	5		
$13.0 < t \leq 14.0$	15		
$14.0 < t \leq 15.0$	18		
$15.0 < t \leq 16.0$	12		

[AQA (SEG) 2000]

2 A sample of households were surveyed. The number of cars owned by each household is shown in the table.

Number of cars owned	Number of households
0	190
1	320
2	393
3	92
4 or more	5

Write down the median number of cars owned by these households.

[AQA (SEG) 2001]

3 The numbers of words in the first 100 sentences of a book are shown in the table.

Number of words	Frequency
1–10	45
11–20	38
21–30	12
31–40	4
41–50	1

Write down the class interval that contains the median.

[AQA (SEG) 2001]

14 Comparing data

When comparing data, you will usually be expected to compare an average (mean, median or mode) and a measure of spread (range or interquartile range).

These are some of the ways that you may be asked to do this:

- from a table
- from two histograms
- from two cumulative frequency diagrams
- from two box plots
- comparing medians and quartile values
- compare data from two different diagrams, e.g. a table and a histogram.

EXAMINER **TIP**
When answering questions that require a comparison, the number of marks will tell you how many comparisons are needed.

When answering a comparison question think about the following points.

- Are the average values different? For example, if you are looking at test scores, does one set of data have a higher average (mean, median or mode) than the other set?

- Is one set of data more spread out than the other set is? For example, if you are looking at heights of boys and girls, is there a bigger difference between the tallest boy's height and the smallest boy's height compared with the difference between the tallest girl's height and the smallest girl's height? Or, is the interquartile range of the boys' heights different from the interquartile range of the girls' heights?

EXAMINER **TIP**
Be careful of extreme or rogue values (sometimes called outliers) at the end of a set of data. These can distort the overall conclusion.

Example 14.1

The table shows the test scores in French for two pupils *A* and *B*. Give two comparisons for this data.

	Mean	Range
A	6.1	17.0
B	9.4	10.2

Solution

Pupil *A* generally scores lower marks. This is shown by a lower mean. Pupil *A* also appears to be less consistent as their scores appear to be spread out more. This is shown by a larger range.

EXAMINER **TIP**
It is not sufficient to just restate the questions, e.g. the mean of *A* is less than the mean of *B*.

It could be that pupil *A* had one really good result that led to a range of 17.0. However, as you do not have the actual scores on each test and you do not know how many tests were taken, you can only comment in general terms about what appears to be most likely.

Example 14.2

The times taken to complete a piece of coursework by two different groups of students are shown in the histograms below. Give two comparisons of the data.

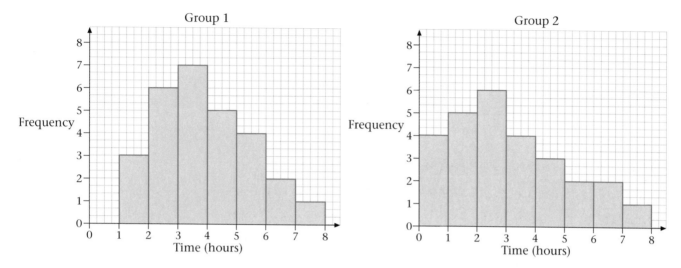

Solution

Group 1 all took over one hour (as there is no bar between 0 and 1) – so the times taken by Group 2 are more spread out. The modal class for Group 1 (frequency of 7) is 3–4 hours but the modal class for Group 2 is 2–3 hours (frequency of 6). This suggests that Group 1 spent more time on average on the coursework than Group 2 did.

Example 14.3

The cumulative frequency curves show the journey times (in minutes) for a student travelling to and from school. Give two comparisons of this data.

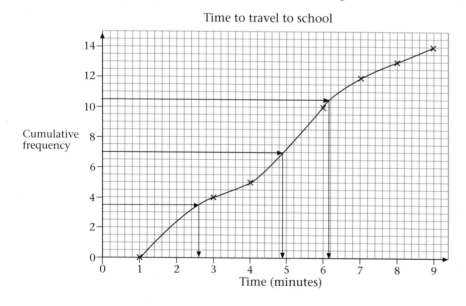

> **Reminder**
> Cumulative frequency curves are covered in Unit 2, Chapter 9 – Cumulative frequency diagrams.

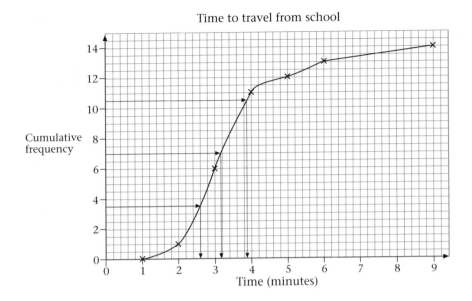

Time to travel from school

Cumulative frequency

Time (minutes)

Solution

A question of this type will usually have earlier parts asking you to find, from a cumulative frequency graph, the median and the interquartile range. You would probably be given the information for the other graph.

Once you have the median and the interquartile range for both graphs, you can then make the comparisons.

The median time taken to travel to school (approximately 4.9 minutes) is longer than the time taken to travel from school (approximately 3.2 minutes). This suggests that it takes longer to travel to school.

The interquartile range for the time taken to travel to school (approximately 3.6) is greater than the interquartile range for the time taken to travel from school (approximately 1.3). This suggests that there is a greater variation in the times taken to travel to school than the times taken to travel from school.

> *Reminder*
> The median is read from the horizontal axis using half the total frequency.

Example 14.4

The box plots show the ages of staff in a school and in a college. Give two comparisons of the data.

Ages of staff

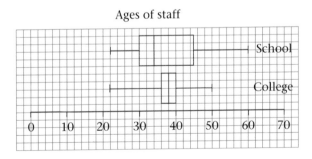

Solution

The median age is lower at the school. This suggests that in general the school has younger staff. Both the range and the interquartile range of the ages of the staff in the school are larger than in the college. This suggests a greater spread in the ages of the staff in the school.

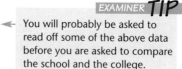

EXAMINER **TIP**

You will probably be asked to read off some of the above data before you are asked to compare the school and the college.

Example 14.5

The table shows data for the number of carrots in a sample of 1 kg bags at two different supermarkets *A* and *B*. Give two comparisons for this data.

	A	*B*
Lower quartile	3	5
Median	9	8
Upper quartile	11	11

Solution

The median is slightly higher at supermarket *A*. This suggests that there are more carrots in a 1 kg bag at supermarket *A*. The interquartile range at *A* is greater than at *B*. This suggests that there is more variation in the numbers of carrots in a 1 kg bag at supermarket *A*.

Practice questions

1 A grocer sells two varieties of tomato. A survey is carried out of the diameters of tomatoes from each variety.

	Mean diameter (cm)	**Range (cm)**
Ripe reds	3.1	4.1
King toms	5.2	1.2

   a Mark says, 'I prefer Ripe reds.' Use the data in the table to give a possible reason why Mark prefers Ripe reds.

   b Jan says, 'I prefer King toms.' Use the data in the table to give a possible reason why Jan prefers King toms.

2 Look at the box plots.

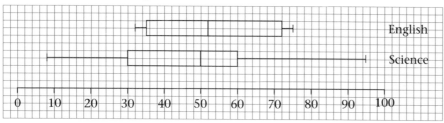

English and Science exam results

Make two comparisons between the data for the Science and English exam results.

Practice exam questions

1 Farmer Jack has two fields. In one field, he plants lettuce seeds by hand. In the other, he plants lettuce seeds using a machine. A sample of lettuce is taken from each field. The diameter of each lettuce is measured; the mean and interquartile range are calculated for each sample. The results are shown in the table.

	Hand	Machine
Mean diameter	15.3 cm	14.7 cm
Interquartile range	3.2 cm	1.2 cm

    a Farmer Jack says, 'It's better to plant by hand.' Using the data given in the table, give a reason to justify his statement.

    b His son Peter says, 'No dad, the machine is better.' Using the data given in the table, give a reason to justify his statement.

                                                         [AQA (NEAB) 2000]

2 Lynne wants to test whether carrots grow better in homemade compost or in coir compost. She grows 30 carrots in each type of compost and measures the length of them when they are three weeks old.

    a Use the data in the table to draw a cumulative frequency curve for the length of carrots grown in homemade compost.

    b Find the median and the interquartile range for the lengths of the carrots grown in homemade compost.

Homemade Compost

Length, l (mm)	Cumulative frequency
< 50	1
< 100	4
< 150	13
< 200	26
< 250	30
< 300	30

The table summarises the results for the carrots grown in coir compost.

    c Draw the cumulative frequency curve for the lengths of the carrots grown in coir compost.

    d Compare the median lengths of the carrots grown in the two types of compost.

Coir Compost

Length of plant, l (mm)	Number of carrots, f
$0 \leqslant l < 50$	1
$50 \leqslant l < 100$	3
$100 \leqslant l < 150$	5
$150 \leqslant l < 200$	12
$200 \leqslant l < 250$	7
$250 \leqslant l < 300$	2

[AQA (SEG) 1998]

15 Single events

This is the basic definition of the probability of an event happening.

$$\text{Probability} = \frac{\text{number of ways that the event can happen}}{\text{total number of outcomes}}$$

Probabilities can only take a value from 0 up to 1 inclusive. They must be written as fractions, decimals or percentages.

Consider throwing a fair dice 100 times and counting how many times a six occurs. You might find that you get 19 sixes out of the 100 throws. You could use this result to give an estimate of the probability of getting a six when you throw the dice.

$$\text{Probability of getting a six} = \frac{\text{number of times that the event happens}}{\text{total number of trials}}$$

$$= \frac{19}{100} \text{ or } 0.19 \text{ or } 19\%$$

This value is called the **relative frequency**. It is based upon one actual experiment. If ten members of your class each carried out this experiment it would be almost certain that each of them would get a different relative frequency. However, if you combined all of the results you would find that the overall relative frequency would tend towards the **theoretical probability**.

When a dice is thrown there are six possible outcomes: 1, 2, 3, 4, 5, and 6. If the dice is **fair** (not biased towards any particular outcome) then there is an equal chance of it landing on any score 1, 2, 3, 4, 5 or 6.

$$\text{Theoretical probability (6)} = \frac{\text{number of ways that the event can happen}}{\text{total number of outcomes}}$$

$$= \frac{1}{6}$$

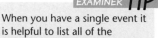

EXAMINER *TIP*

◄ When you have a single event it is helpful to list all of the outcomes so that you can calculate the probability of a particular event happening.

Similarly the probability of the dice landing on a four is $\frac{1}{6}$, or probability of the dice landing on a one is $\frac{1}{6}$.

Example 15.1

A fair spinner has five equal sections: two are red, one is white, one is black and one is yellow. The spinner is spun once. Find the probability that the spinner lands on:

a white b red c *not* yellow d green.

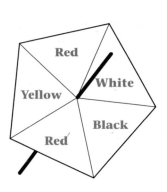

Solution

The spinner is fair, so there is an equal chance of landing on each section. Often a short-hand notation is used; the probability of an event A can therefore be written as P (A).

a There is one white section and so one way that the spinner could land on white.

$$P(W) = \frac{1}{5}$$

b There are two red sections on the spinner therefore two ways that the spinner could land on red.

$$P(R) = \frac{2}{5}$$

c The sum of all the probabilities of all possible outcomes is one. When the spinner is spun it will either land on yellow or it won't, i.e. it will land on another colour. The sum of the probabilities of it landing on yellow and not landing on yellow must equal 1. To find the probability of an event not happening you can use this formula:

$$P(A \text{ happens}) + P(A \text{ not happening}) = 1$$

$$P(A \text{ not happening}) = 1 - P(A \text{ happens})$$

$$P(\text{not } Y) = 1 - P(Y)$$
$$= 1 - \frac{1}{5}$$
$$= \frac{4}{5}$$

d There are no green sections on the spinner.

$$P(G) = 0$$

Practice questions

1 A fair standard six-sided dice is thrown once. Write down the probability of the following events happening.

  a The dice lands on the number 5.

  b The dice lands on the number 2.

  c The dice lands on an even number.

  d The dice lands on an odd number.

  e The dice lands on a prime number.

  f The dice lands on the number 8.

2 A standard pack of 52 playing cards is shuffled. One card is picked at random from the pack. Find the probability that the card picked is:

  a the King of Hearts   **e** a Jack

  b the Ace of Spades   **f** a picture card (King, Queen or Jack)

  c the 8 of Diamonds   **g** a number card

  d the King or Queen of Clubs   **h** a red card.

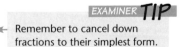
EXAMINER *TIP*

Remember to cancel down fractions to their simplest form.

Practice exam question

1 a Copy the probability scale. Estimate the probability of each of the following events and mark the letter on the probability scale.

0   1

   A A fair coin lands heads.

   B A household chosen at random has a television set.

   C The first person to leave a college today will be left handed.

b Which of these three events has a probability called 50/50?

c Write down an example of an impossible event.

d Write down an example of an event that is certain to happen.

[AQA (SEG) 1998]

16 Outcomes for two successive events

A number of probability questions will involve listing outcomes for two successive events, e.g. throwing two coins, spinning two spinners, throwing a coin and spinning a spinner. In the exam, you will usually be given a blank or part filled two-way table and you will be asked to complete all the possible outcomes for that experiment.

Example 16.1

Peter is playing a game. For each go he spins two fair triangular spinners, one blue and one red, each numbered 1, 2 and 3.

The numbers that the spinners land on are *added* together to give the score for that go.

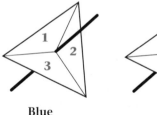

Blue   Red

a Complete the table to show all the possible scores.

		Red spinner		
		1	2	3
	1	2	3	4
Blue spinner	2			
	3			

b In one go, find the probability of getting a score of:

  i six   **ii** four   **iii** seven.

c Peter needs to get a total of *10 or more* in two goes to win the game. List all the pairs of scores that will give a total of 10 or more in two goes.

First score						
Second score						

[AQA (SEG) 2001]

Solution

a You are told in the question that you have to *add* the numbers that each spinner lands on to get a score. In one go, the blue spinner could land on the number 1 and the red spinner could also land on the number 1. So the score would be 1 + 1 = 2. Or, blue lands on 1 and red lands on 2 so the score is 1 + 2 = 3. Or, blue lands on 1 and red lands on 3 so the score would be 1 + 3 = 4. These scores are shown in the first row of the table. The other possible scores are found by considering the other numbers that the two spinners land on.

		Red spinner		
		1	2	3
	1	2	3	4
Blue spinner	2	3	4	5
	3	4	5	6

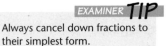
EXAMINER **TIP**
A two-way table will identify all the options for you.

b Since the spinners were both fair, each of the scores in the table are equally likely to occur. There are nine possible scores in the table.

  i There is 1 way of scoring 6.

$$P(6) \text{ is } \frac{\text{number of ways of scoring 6}}{\text{total number of possible scores}} = \frac{1}{9}$$

  ii There are 3 ways of scoring a 4.

EXAMINER **TIP**
Always cancel down fractions to their simplest form.

$$P(4) = \frac{3}{9} = \frac{1}{3}$$

  iii There is no way of scoring a 7.

$$P(7) = 0$$

c Every time Peter has a go he will get one of the scores shown in the two-way table. He needs to get a total of *10 or more* in two goes. In one go, Peter's biggest possible score is 6. To get a total of 10 or more he must then get either a 6, 5, or 4 on his second go. List these in the table.

EXAMINER **TIP**
Often the number of rows given in a table suggests how many ways there are to answer that part of the question.

Only three columns have been filled, so it may be that there are more possible answers. Getting a 6 on the first go and then a 5 on the second go is not the same as getting a 5 on the first go and then getting a 6 on the second go. So you can now add (5, 6) and (4, 6) to the table leaving just one more column. The only other way of scoring 10 or more is by getting a 5 on the first go and then a 5 on the second.

First score	6	6	6	5	4	5
Second score	6	5	4	6	6	5

Example 16.2

A game is played by throwing a fair coin and a fair six-sided dice. When the coin lands tails, the score is the amount shown on the dice. When the coin lands heads, the score is *double* the amount shown on the dice.

a Complete the table showing all possible scores.

b Sahima throws the coin and the dice once. Calculate the probability that Sahima gets:

   i a score of ten   ii an even score   iii a score less than five.

		Dice					
		1	2	3	4	5	6
Coin	Tails						
	Heads						

c John plays the game 30 times. How many times would you expect him to score more than 3?

[AQA (SEG) 1998]

Solution

A coin and a dice are thrown. The outcome of the coin determines the possible scores that you can get in this game.

a If the coin lands on tails, the score is the amount shown on the dice. So the top row of the two-way table must have scores exactly the same as the amount shown on the dice, i.e. if the coin lands tails and the dice shows the number 1 the score is 1.

		Dice					
		1	2	3	4	5	6
Coin	Tails	1	2	3	4	5	6
	Heads	2	4	6	8	10	12

If the coin lands on heads you have to double the amount shown on the dice. So if the coin lands on heads and the dice shows the number 1 the score is 2 (2 × 1). The rows of the table are therefore filled in as shown.

b Since the coin and the dice are both fair the outcomes (scores) listed in the two-way table are equally likely to occur. There are 12 possible outcomes. Use the table to find the number of ways each event can occur.

  i   There is one way to score 10.

$$P(10) = \frac{1}{12}$$

  ii   There are nine ways of scoring an even number.

$$P(\text{even score}) = \frac{9}{12} = \frac{3}{4}$$

  iii   There are six ways of scoring less than 5, i.e. scoring a 1, 2, 3 or 4.

$$P(\text{score } 5) = \frac{6}{12} = \frac{1}{2}$$

c You can use the probability of an event to calculate the expected number of outcomes of that event for a set number of trials. Firstly work out the probability of a score of more than 3.

$$P \text{ (score more than 3)} = \frac{8}{12} = \frac{2}{3}$$

John plays this game 30 times and the chance of him getting a score of more than 3 is $\frac{2}{3}$. To work out the expected number of times an event can happen use this formula.

Expectation = probability × number of trials

$$= \frac{2}{3} \times 30 = 20$$

So you would expect John to score more than 3 twenty times in a total of 30 trials.

Practice questions

1 Simon and Sarah plan to have three children. They know that each child is equally likely to be a boy (B) or a girl (G).

a Copy the table and list the possible outcomes for the sexes of the three children.

First child	Second child	Third child

b What is the probability that the first two children are boys and the third child is a girl?

c What is the probability that there will be two boys and one girl in the family of three children?

[AQA (SEG) 2000]

2 In a board game, two fair six-sided dice are thrown. The total score is the sum of the two numbers shown on the dice.

   a Copy and complete the table showing all the possible total scores.

Dice 1

		1	2	3	4	5	6
	1						
	2						
Dice 2	3						
	4						
	5						
	6						

   b John throws the pair of dice once.

   i   Calculate the probability that John scores a total of 5.

   ii What is the most likely score?

   c John throws the pair of dice 180 times. Calculate the number of times he would expect to get a total score of 12.   [AQA (SEG) 1997]

Practice exam question

1 A fair coin is thrown and a fair dice is rolled. If the coin shows heads, the score is the number shown on the dice. If the coin shows tails, the score is double the number shown on the dice.

   a Copy and complete the table to show each possible score.

Dice

		1	2	3	4	5	6
Coin	Tails			6			
	Heads	1					

   b What is the probability of getting a score of 10?

   c What is the probability of getting a score of less than 6?   [AQA 2002]

17 Mutually exclusive events

When two events are **mutually exclusive** they cannot happen at the same time. For example, Adam, Billie and Chris are the only people playing a game where there is only one winner. The three possible outcomes – Adam wins the game, Billie wins the game, Chris wins the game – are mutually exclusive events as any two of them cannot happen at the same time. If there has to be one winner then the probabilities of these three events must now sum to one (it is certain that one of them wins the game).

P (A) + P (B) + P (C) = 1

Calculating the missing probability

You may be given some probabilities for mutually exclusive events and asked to find a missing probability.

Example 17.1

The table shows the probabilities that Ian listens to a CD, a tape or the radio while he is doing his homework.

Listens to	Probability
CD	0.42
Tape	0.25
Radio	0.10

What is the probability that Ian does *not* listen to a CD, a tape or the radio while he is doing his homework tonight?

[AQA (SEG) 2000]

Solution

You have to assume that either Ian *does* listen to a CD, a tape or the radio or he *does not* listen to any of them while he is doing his homework that night. These are the possible events, so the sum of the probability of these events must be 1.

P (does listen) + P (does not listen) = 1

$$P \text{ (does not listen)} = 1 - P \text{ (does listen)}$$

$$= 1 - [\, P \text{ (CD)} + P \text{ (Tape)} + P \text{ (Radio)}]$$

$$= 1 - (0.42 + 0.25 + 0.10)$$

$$= 1 - 0.77$$

$$= 0.23$$

Addition law for mutually exclusive events

If two events are mutually exclusive, and so neither of them can happen at the same time, the probability of either one or the other of them happening must be the sum of the individual probabilities of either of them happening. This is the addition law for mutually exclusive events and can be written as follows.

P (A *or* B) = P (A) + P (B)

Example 17.2

A hospital carried out a survey about how patients keep appointments. They calculated the following probabilities.

	Probability
Patient arrives early	0.40
Patient arrives on time	0.25
Patient arrives late	0.23
Patient misses appointment	

It is certain that the patient will do one of the four options.

a   Calculate the probability that a patient arrives early or is on time for an appointment.

b   Calculate the probability that a patient misses an appointment.   [AQA (SEG) 1999]

Solution

A patient either arrives early, on time, late or misses an appointment. They are mutually exclusive events.

a   Use the addition law to find the probability that a patient either arrives early or is on time.

P (arrives early *or* is on time) = P (arrives early) + P (is on time)

$$= 0.40 + 0.25$$

$$= 0.65$$

b   It is certain that the patient will do one of the four options, hence the sum of the probabilities of all the events is 1.

P (misses appointment) = 1 – P (does not miss appointment)

$$= 1 - P \text{ (arrives early or on time or late)}$$

$$= 1 - (0.40 + 0.25 + 0.23)$$

$$= 1 - 0.88$$

$$= 0.12$$

Practice question

1 A four-sided spinner has sides numbered 1, 2, 3 and 4. The spinner is biased. The table shows the probability of the spinner landing on each number.

Number	Probability
1	0.10
2	0.15
3	0.45
4	0.30

What is the probability that the spinner will land on 3 *or* 4?

[AQA (SEG) 2000]

Practice exam questions

1 Josh always eats one piece of fruit for his lunch. This is either an apple, a pear, an orange or a banana. The table shows some of the probabilities for the fruit that Josh eats.

Fruit	Probability
Apple	0.45
Pear	0.10
Orange	0.15
Banana	

  a What is the probability that Josh eats an apple *or* a pear for lunch?

  b What is the probability that Josh eats a banana for lunch?   [AQA (SEG) 2001]

2 A computer generates numbers at random. In a test run, the computer generated the following numbers.

  2 5 7 3 11 12 14 15 3 7 4 6 4 1 10 9 12 5 1 13

  a Use the test run to estimate the probability of the computer generating an even number.

  b Use your answer to **a** to calculate how many even numbers you would expect when the computer generates 300 numbers at random.

The table shows three different events and their probabilities.

Event	Description	Probability
A	An odd number is generated	$\frac{9}{17}$
B	A multiple of 4 is generated	$\frac{3}{17}$
C	A prime number is generated	$\frac{7}{17}$

  c Calculate the probability of event A *or* event B occurring when a number is generated.

  d Explain why the probability of event A *or* event C occurring is not $\frac{16}{17}$.   [AQA (SEG) 1997]

18 Tree diagrams

Tree diagrams are a useful way of illustrating the possible outcomes of two or more events. Always draw large clear diagrams that show the probabilities on the branches and the outcomes at the end of the branches. Below is a tree diagram showing the outcomes for tossing a coin twice.

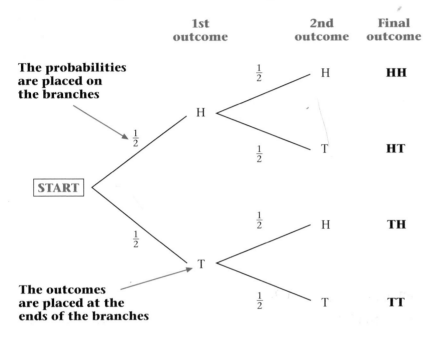

The probabilities are placed on the branches

The outcomes are placed at the ends of the branches

You go along the tree branches from the Start box to arrive at the final outcome, e.g. moving along the top two branches shows a Head as the first outcome and a Head as the second outcome; the final outcome would be HH. To calculate the probability of two independent events, occurring one after the other, use this formula.

P (A *and* B) = P (A) × P (B)

This is called the multiplication law for independent events. The probability of getting two heads one after the other can therefore be calculated as follows.

$$P (H \text{ } and \text{ } H) = \frac{1}{2} \times \frac{1}{2} = \frac{1}{4}$$

Points to remember:

● the probabilities on each pair of branches must always sum to 1

● multiply the probabilities as you move along the branches

● the sum of all the probabilities of all of the final outcomes must always sum to 1.

Example 18.1

In Mathematics exams, some candidates arrive without calculators or rulers. The tree diagram shows the probability for each event.

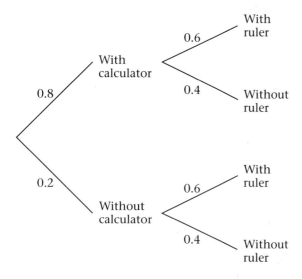

a Calculate the probability that a candidate arrives at an exam with a calculator *and* without a ruler.

b 100 candidates arrive for a Mathematics exam. How many candidates would you *expect* to arrive without a calculator *and* without a ruler?

[AQA (SEG) 1999]

Solution

a Look at the first pair of branches on the tree diagram. These show the probabilities for a student arriving with or without a calculator. The second pairs of branches show the probabilities for a students arriving with or without a ruler. Go along the first set to see the probability for arriving with a calculator (0.8), and then along the connecting branch (in the second set) to see the probability for arriving without a ruler (0.4). Use the multiplication law for independent events.

P (with calculator *and* without ruler) = P (with calc.) × P (without ruler)

$$= 0.8 \times 0.4$$

$$= 0.32$$

b First find the probability of a candidate arriving without a calculator *and* without a ruler.

P (no calc. *and* no ruler) = P (no calc.) × P (no ruler)

$$= 0.2 \times 0.4$$

$$= 0.08$$

Use the probability to find how many students you would expect to arrive without a calculator and without a ruler in a sample of 100 candidates.

Expectation = probability × total number of trials

$$= 0.08 \times 100$$

$$= 8$$

You would expect 8 out of 100 candidates to arrive at an exam without a calculator *and* without a ruler.

Here you are given a tree diagram. You should be able to draw your own tree diagrams to help you answer questions when no tree diagram is given.

Example 18.2

A bag contains three red, four blue and two white discs. A disc is taken at random from the bag, its colour is noted and it is then replaced in the bag. Another disc is then taken at random from the bag and its colour is noted.

a Draw a fully labelled tree diagram to illustrate this situation.

b Calculate the probability that the two discs are the same colour.

Solution

a You have to draw a tree diagram. Firstly give yourself plenty of space and use a ruler to draw the branches of the tree diagram. Since there are three possible colours to be selected both the first time and second time you will have 9 (3 × 3) possible outcomes. The question said to draw a *fully labelled* tree diagram so you need to add the probabilities to each branch.

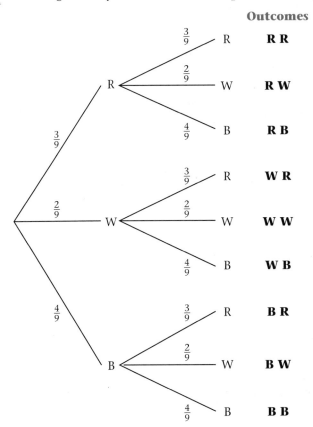

Outcomes

EXAMINER **TIP**

It is often a good idea to list the outcomes at the end of the branches; this will help you see all the possible outcomes more clearly.

b Calculate the probability that the two discs are the same colour. This covers the outcomes RR, BB, WW. These are three mutually exclusive outcomes so you can use the addition rule. First you must find the probability of each of these outcomes. RR, BB and WW are all two independent selections so you use the multiplication law.

$$P(RR) = \frac{3}{9} \times \frac{3}{9} \qquad\qquad P(BB) = \frac{4}{9} \times \frac{4}{9} \qquad\qquad P(WW) = \frac{2}{9} \times \frac{2}{9}$$

$$= \frac{9}{81} \qquad\qquad\qquad = \frac{16}{81} \qquad\qquad\qquad = \frac{4}{81}$$

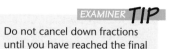

EXAMINER **TIP**

◄ Do not cancel down fractions until you have reached the final answer.

$$P(\text{same colour}) = P(RR) + P(BB) + P(WW)$$

$$= \frac{9}{81} + \frac{16}{81} + \frac{4}{81}$$

$$= \frac{29}{81}$$

Practice exam questions

1 Jane runs in two races. The probability that she wins her first race is $\frac{1}{3}$. The probability that she wins her second race is $\frac{1}{4}$.

   a Draw a fully labelled tree diagram showing the possible outcomes for Jane's races.

   b Calculate the probability that Jane wins both races.

   c Calculate the probability that Jane wins only one of her races.   [AQA (SEG) 1999]

2 Mrs Choudbury visits two shops that sell cards.

   The probability that she buys a card in the first shop is 0.2.

   The probability that she buys a card in the second shop is 0.3.

   a Draw a fully labelled probability tree diagram.

   b Calculate the probability that Mrs Choudbury does not buy a card in either shop.   [AQA (SEG) 2001]

3 Greg has a fair spinner with five equal sections.

   Three sections are red and two are blue.

   He spins the spinner twice.

   a Draw a fully labelled probability tree diagram to show the outcomes.

   b Calculate the probability that the spinner lands on red both times.   [AQA 2002]

19 Comparing experimental and theoretical probability

Experimental probability is probability based on the results of carrying out trials. You can use experimental probability to test for bias.

$$\text{Experimental probability} = \frac{\text{number of successful trials}}{\text{total number of trials}}$$

When carrying out an experiment, it is usually assumed that a greater number of trials will result in the probabilities calculated being more reliable.

Theoretical probability looks at equally likely events such as: rolling a dice, throwing a coin, spinning a spinner or choosing a counter from a bag. It is used to predict what is likely to happen.

$$\text{Theoretical probability} = \frac{\text{number of successful outcomes}}{\text{total number of outcomes}}$$

You may be asked to compare data taken from an experiment with the results obtained from the theoretical probabilities in order to decide whether there is bias.

> **Reminder**
> If an event is biased towards a particular outcome, it is more likely that the outcome will happen than any one of the other possible outcomes.

> **Reminder**
> Probabilities must be a fraction, decimal or percentage.

Example 19.1

A six-sided dice was rolled 30 times. A score of 2 was obtained nine times. Do you think that the dice is biased?

Give a reason for your answer.

Solution

Calculate the experimental and theoretical probabilities so you can compare them.

Experimental probability of obtaining a 2 is $\frac{9}{30} = 0.3$

Theoretical probability of obtaining a 2 is $\frac{1}{6} = 0.17$

Over 30 trials the experimental probability of obtaining a 2 is almost twice the theoretical probability. You could say from these results that the dice was biased towards obtaining a 2.

Example 19.2

Here are four methods that can be used to estimate probabilities.

- Method A – A calculation based on equally likely outcomes.

- Method B – A calculation based on the results of a survey or questionnaire.

- Method C – A calculation based on the results of an experiment.

- Method D – A calculation based on past records.

Which method A, B, C or D is the most appropriate for estimating the probability of each of the following events?

a   A weighted six-sided dice lands on an odd number.

b   A 50-year-old male shopper will buy a particular product.

c   A pupil will be top in a test.

d   A fair spinner lands on red.

Solution

a   Method C; if you performed an experiment with a large number of trials, you could calculate the experimental probability of the dice landing on an odd number.

b   Method B; if you carried out a survey you could calculate how likely it is that a person in this category would buy the product.

c   Method D; if you looked at the previous results you could estimate how likely the pupil is to be top in the test.

d   Method A; since the spinner is fair, you can use equally likely outcomes to estimate the probability of it landing on red.

Practice questions

1   A coin is thrown 20 times. It lands on heads nine times. Write down:

a   the experimental probability of landing on heads

b   the experimental probability of landing on tails

c   the theoretical probability of landing on heads

d   the theoretical probability of landing on tails.

2   Look at the four methods of estimating probability in Example 19.2. Which method is most appropriate for estimating the probability of the following events?

a   A fair six-sided dice lands on the number 6.

b   A weighted (or biased) coloured spinner lands on a particular colour.

c   A pupil passes their GCSE Mathematics examination.

Practice exam questions

1 Listed below are four methods that can be used for estimating probabilities.

- Method A: A calculation based on equally likely outcomes.

- Method B: A calculation based on the results of a survey.

- Method C: A calculation based on the results of an experiment.

- Method D: A calculation based on results from past records.

   Which method is most appropriate for estimating the probability of each of the following events?

   a Shoppers would use a suggested new bus service.

   b A fair coin will land showing heads.

   c A weighted coin will land showing heads.

   d Sami will be late for school tomorrow.   [AQA (SEG) 2000]

2 Four methods of estimating probabilities are listed below.

- Method A: A calculation based on the results of a survey.

- Method B: A calculation based on the results of an experiment.

- Method C: A calculation based on the results from past data.

- Method D: A calculation based on equally likely outcomes.

   Choose the most appropriate method for estimating the following probabilities.

   a Ted's horse will win its next race.

   b Supermarket shoppers will buy a new brand of toothpaste.

   c You will win the first prize in a raffle at your school fair.   [AQA (SEG) 2001]

3 An international survey found the probability of being left-handed is 0.09.

   a What is the probability of being right-handed?

   b The table shows the results of a class survey.

	Boys	Girls
Left-handed	1	2
Right-handed	12	10

   i   A child is chosen at random from the class. What is the probability that the child is left-handed?

   ii Give a reason why the results of the class survey are different from the international survey.   [AQA (SEG) 1999]

20 Relative frequency

Relative frequency compares the actual number of successful trials to the total number of trials in an experiment. It is often used as an estimate of probability.

In the exam, you could be asked to use either a table showing the results of successive trials or a graph of the results to estimate probabilities, or to comment on the reliability of the results.

The most important point when commenting about reliability is that the more trials that are undertaken in the experiment the more likely it is that the relative frequency will approach or be close to the value of the theoretical probability.

You may be asked to calculate the relative frequency, or you may be asked to use the relative frequency to calculate the number of times you expect something to happen in a given number of trials.

Example 20.1

A fair dice is rolled ten times. It lands on the number 2 three times. Write down the relative frequency of it landing on the number 2.

Solution

Relative frequency of landing on the number 2 is $\frac{3}{10} = 0.3$

Example 20.2

The relative frequency of a dice landing on the number 6 is found to be 0.2. The dice is rolled 100 times. How many times would you expect it to land on the number 6?

Solution

The relative frequency tells us that $\frac{1}{5}$ ($0.2 = \frac{1}{5}$) of the time we can expect the dice to land on the number 6.

Expectation = relative frequency × number of trials

$$= 0.2 \times 100$$

$$= 20$$

We can expect the dice to land on the number 6 twenty times in 100 trials.

Example 20.3

A five-sided spinner is spun. The table shows the relative frequencies of landing on white.

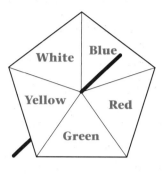

Number of spins	Relative frequency of landing on white
20	0.25
50	0.18
100	0.21

a How many times did the spinner land on white in the first 20 spins?

b Estimate the relative frequency of landing on white in the first 20 spins after 200 spins.

Solution

a Number of times that spinner landed on white in the first 20 spins is
$0.25 \times 20 = 5$

b The most reliable estimate is for the greatest number of spins. Use the relative frequency of landing on white after 100 spins to estimate that the relative frequency after 200 spins will be 0.21.

Example 20.4

A bag contains 100 coloured counters. A counter is picked at random and then replaced. The relative frequency of getting a blue counter is calculated after 10, 25 and 50 goes.

The results are shown on the graph. Work out the number of blue counters after:

a 10 goes

b 25 goes

c 50 goes

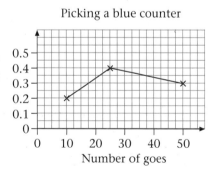

Picking a blue counter

Solution

a Reading off at 10, the relative frequency is 0.2, so that the number of blue counters is: $10 \times 0.2 = 2$ blue counters.

b Reading off at 25, the relative frequency is 0.4, so that the number of blue counters is: $25 \times 0.4 = 10$ blue counters.

c Reading off at 50, the relative frequency is 0.3, so that the number of blue counters is: $50 \times 0.3 = 15$ blue counters.

Practice questions

1 A dice is thrown 50 times. The relative frequency of getting a 6 is calculated every ten throws. The results are shown on the graph.

   Work out the number of sixes after:

   a 10 throws

   b 20 throws

   c 30 throws

   d 40 throws

   e 50 throws

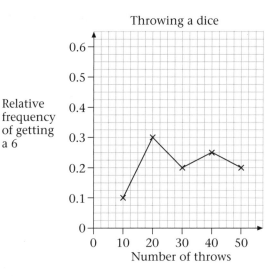

Throwing a dice

2 A coloured spinner is spun 100 times. Here are the results. Copy and complete the table of relative frequencies.

Number of spins	10	20	50	100
Number of times the spinner lands on red	3	8	15	32
Relative frequency of landing on red	0.3			

   Write down the best estimate of the probability of the spinner landing on red. Explain your answer.

Practice exam questions

1 A dice has four faces: a red face, a blue face, a yellow face and a green face. It is suspected that the dice is biased towards landing on the red face. These are the results of the first five throws: red, blue, red, yellow and red.

   a Use these results to calculate the relative frequency of the dice landing on the red face in the first five throws.

   The graph shows the relative frequency of the dice landing on the red face in the first 20 throws.

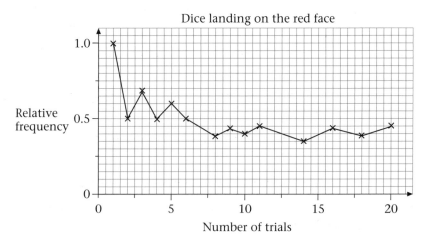

Dice landing on the red face

b Use the graph to estimate the probability of the dice landing on the red face:

   i   using the results of the first 10 throws

   ii   using the results of the first 20 throws.

The dice is equally likely to land on the blue, yellow or green face. In 100 throws it landed on the red face 43 times.

c Estimate the probability of the dice landing on the green face.   [AQA (SEG) 1998]

2 Emily makes a spinner with different coloured sections. She does an experiment to find an estimate for the probability that the spinner lands on *red*.

She spins it 150 times.

She records her results and calculates the relative frequency at various stages of the experiment. The graph shows the relative frequency against the number of spins so far.

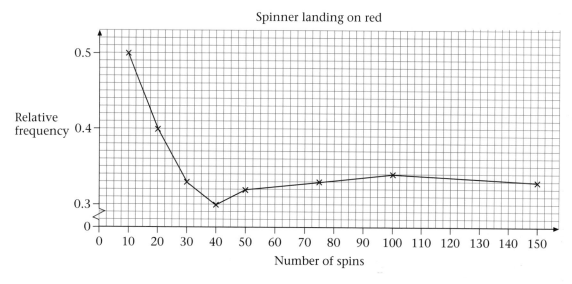

Spinner landing on red

a Use the graph to calculate the number of reds obtained in the first 20 spins.

b Should the graph be used to find the number of reds obtained in the first 15 spins? Give a reason for your answer.

c What does the graph show about the relative frequency as the number of spins increase?

d Emily's experiment confirms that her spinner is fair. The spinner has six coloured sections of equal shape and size.

   i   How many sections are coloured red? Give a reason for your answer.

   ii   Emily spins the spinner two more times. What is the theoretical probability that she gets red both times?   [AQA (NEAB) 2000]

Practice exam paper

Section A Calculator 25 minutes

Total of 20 marks for section A

1 In a board game a pair of fair six-sided dice are thrown.

   The total score is the sum of the two numbers shown on the dice.

   a Complete the table showing all the possible total scores.

Dice 1

	1	2	3	4	5	6
1						
2						
3						
4						
5						
6						

Dice 2 (rows 3)

(2 marks)

   Geoff throws the pair of dice once.

   b i Work out the probability that Geoff scores a total of six.

   ....

   Answer .... *(1 mark)*

   ii Write down the most likely total score.

   ....

   Answer .... *(1 mark)*

Jim throws the pair of dice 120 times.

   c Calculate the number of times he would expect a total score of ten.

   ....

   ....

   Answer .... *(2 marks)*

2 The following goods were sold by a shop in one week.

Eye colour	Number of students	Angle (°)
Blue	252	
Brown	126	
Green	108	
Hazel	54	

The data in the table is to be represented by a pie chart.

a Calculate the angles for each sector and insert them into the column in the table.

....

....

....

.... *(2 marks)*

b Draw the pie chart.

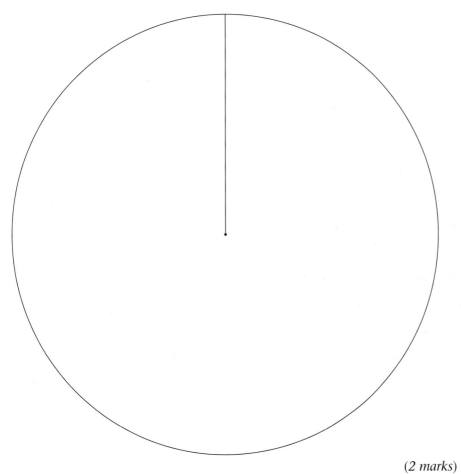

(2 marks)

3 Here are the numbers of passengers on the Popples bus for 11 different journeys.

14   17   13   22   25   8   19   20   26   7   6

a Complete the stem and leaf diagram

KEY: ... | ... represents 13 passengers

0 | ....
1 | ....
2 | ....   (3 marks)

b How many journeys had more than ten passengers?

....

Answer ....   (1 mark)

c What was the median number of passengers?

....

Answer ....   (1 mark)

d On the next bus journey there were 27 passengers. What is the new median number of passengers?

....

....

Answer ....   (1 mark)

4 The table shows the age distribution of 80 shoppers in a supermarket.

Age, x (years)	Number of shoppers
$15 \leqslant x < 20$	14
$20 \leqslant x < 25$	20
$25 \leqslant x < 30$	16
$30 \leqslant x < 35$	20
$35 \leqslant x < 40$	10

Calculate an estimate of the mean age of the shoppers.

....

....

....

....

....

Answer ....   (4 marks)

Section B   Non calculator   25 minutes

Total of 20 marks for section B

5   A bag contains four red, three blue and five yellow counters.

A counter is picked from the bag at random.

Find the probability that the counter picked from the bag is:

a   blue

....

                Answer   ....   (*2 marks*)

b   yellow

....

                Answer   ....   (*2 marks*)

c   *not* red

....

                Answer   ....   (*1 mark*)

6   The table shows the screen size of different televisions and the price.

Screen size (inch)	24	28	24	32	36	32	36
Price (£)	250	350	275	500	650	475	700

a   Plot a scatter graph of the data.   (*2 marks*)

b   Draw the line of best fit   (*1 mark*)

c   Describe the relationship between the screen size of the television and its
    price.

....

                Answer   ....   (*1 mark*)

d Explain why it may not be appropriate to use the graph to estimate the price of a television with a screen size of 42 inches.

....

....

.... *(1 mark)*

Price (£)

700 —

600 —

500 —

400 —

300 —

200 —

0 —

0   22   24   26   28   30   32   34   36

Screen size (inches)

7 There are 900 pupils in a school.

The probability that a pupil catches the school bus is 0.6

Calculate the number of pupils you would expect to catch the school bus.

....

Answer .... *(2 marks)*

8 The speeds (in miles per hour) of 200 cars travelling on a motorway are recorded.

The results are shown on the cumulative frequency diagram.

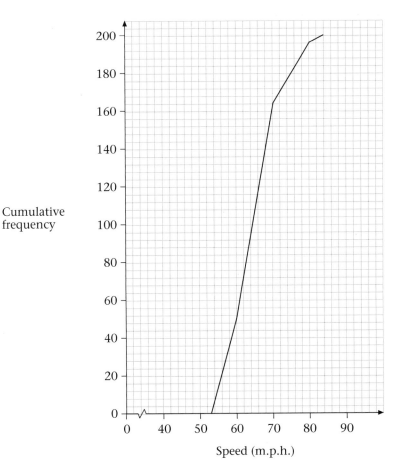

Cumulative frequency

Speed (m.p.h.)

a Use the graph to find:

i the median speed

....

Answer .... *(1 mark)*

ii the interquartile range.

....

....

Answer .... *(2 marks)*

b The speed limit is 70 m.p.h.

How many cars were breaking the speed limit?

....

Answer .... *(2 marks)*

c The slowest car was travelling at 53 m.p.h.

The fastest car was travelling at 84 m.p.h.

Use this information and part **a** to draw a box plot.

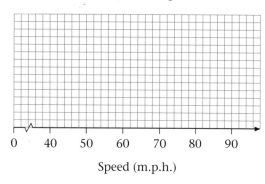

Speed (m.p.h.)

(3 marks)

Answers

1 Questionnaires

Practice exam questions
1 Question 1: Not all ages are covered. Question 2: The answers 5, 10 and 20 can be given in more than one response section.
2 **a** For example: Do you exercise outside school? Do you play any sports?
 b Sample is biased towards girls. Sample is biased towards people who play netball or sport.
 c **i** It is a leading question – 'don't you agree' leads you to agree with the statement.
  ii The responder cannot reply 'no'. Also the responses 'occasionally', 'sometimes' and 'usually' are too vague.

2 Two-way tables

Practice questions
1 **a**

Amount earned (£)	Tally	Frequency
0.00 to 9.99	ĦĦ ĦĦ ĦĦ I	16
10.00 to 19.99	ĦĦ ĦĦ ĦĦ ĦĦ III	23
20.00 to 29.99	ĦĦ	5
30.00 to 39.99	IIII	4
40.00 or over	II	2

 b The modal class is £10.00 to £19.99.
 c **i** No mention of time period.
  ii The word 'work' is too vague, or it is an open question.
2 **a** Taxi B **b** 12 **c** 114

Practice exam question
1 **a** 14 **b** 5 **c** 16 **d** 49

3 Pie charts

Practice questions
1 **a** Maths = 90°, Science = 105°, French = 45°, English = 60°, Art = 60°
 b Blue = 60°, Red = 180°, Green = 20°, Yellow = 40°, Other = 60°
2 **a** True Pigs = 120° (one-third of 360°)
 b False Goats + Cows (105°) is less than Sheep (135°)
 c False Cows (60°) is not twice Goats (45°)
 d False Sheep + Goats = 180°

Practice exam questions
1 **a**

Item	Value (£)	Angle (°)
Umbrellas	350	100
Wellington boots	560	160
Gloves	123	35
Hats	155	44
Scarves	72	21
Total	1260	360

 b A pie chart with the above angles.

2 Baths and showers = 60°, Washing machine = 44°, Flushing toilet = 116°, Other = 140°

4 Averages

Practice question
1 **a** Mode = 5 Median = 6 Mean = 7 Range = 11
 b Mode = 6 Median = 4 Mean = 5 Range = 12
 c Mode = 5 Median = 5.5 Mean = 6 Range = 7
 d Mode = 3 Median = 5.5 Mean = 5.25 Range = 6

Practice exam questions
1 **a** Range = 14 minutes **b** Mean = 4.7 minutes
2 Median = 24.2 seconds

5 Stem and leaf diagrams

Practice questions
1 **a**   Key: 3 | 7 represents 37 passengers

```
3 | 7 7 9
4 | 1 1 2 5 8
5 | 1 3
```

 b Range = 16 passengers
2 **a** Range = 25 fish **b** Mode = 0 fish **c** Median = 5 fish
 d Interquartile range = 16 fish
 e The median will increase (to 5.5) as the middle values will then be 5 & 6.
3 **a**   Key: 1 | 9 represents 19

```
0 | 2 4 8 9
1 | 0 1 1 2 4 5 6 8 9
2 | 0 0 1 2 3
```

 b 5.5

Practice exam questions
1 **a** 4 **b** 20
 c   Key: 4 | 3 represents 43

```
0 | 9
1 | 0 2 2 6 7 8
2 | 0 3 3 5 6 9
3 | 2 7
4 | 3
```

 Median = 21.5

6 Frequency diagrams

Practice questions
1

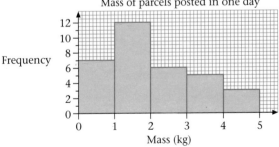

Mass of parcels posted in one day

2

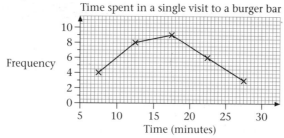

Time spent in a single visit to a burger bar

3

Weight (g)	Tally	Frequency
450 to less than 452	JHT II	7
452 to less than 454	JHT	5
454 to less than 456	III	3
456 to less than 458	IIII	4
458 to less than 460	I	1

b

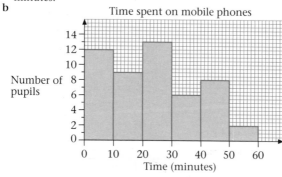

Weight of tomato sauce samples

c Valid answers include: Yes, because none of the bottles contain less than the marked weight. No, because some bottles contain well over the marked weight.

Practice exam questions

1 a Modal class is 20 minutes or more but less than 30 minutes.

b

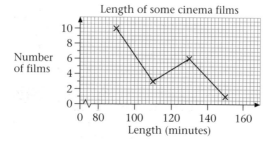

Time spent on mobile phones

2

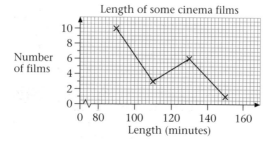

Length of some cinema films

7 Line graphs (time series)

Practice questions

1 a

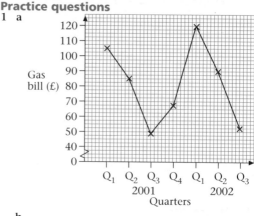

b

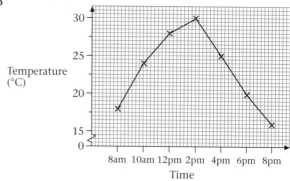

Practice exam questions

1 a

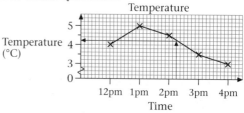

Temperature

b i 4.2 °C
 ii The temperature was not monitored at 2.15 pm.

2 a i The horizontal scale is not linear.
 ii The vertical scale does not start from zero.

8 Scatter graphs

Practice questions

1 a & c See graph   **b** Positive   **d** Estimate = 41.

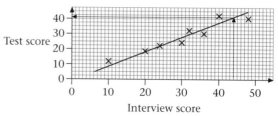

Scores of interview candidates

2 a & **c** See graph   **b** Positive   **d** Estimate = 22 500 offences

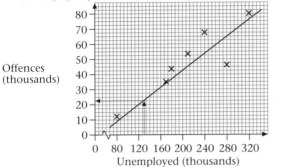

e The extrapolation will not be accurate as the figure is outside the range of the data already collected.

Practice exam questions

1 a & **c** See graph   **b** Positive   **d** Estimate is 84.

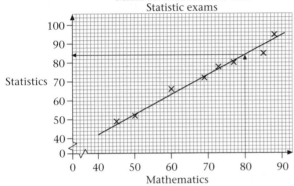

Marks for Mathematics and Statistic exams

2 a & **c** See graph   **b** Positive   **d** Estimate is £170.

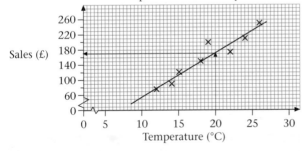

Sales and maximum daytime temperature on Saturdays

9 Cumulative frequency diagrams

Practice questions

1 a

Annual business mileage	Number of sales people
less than 10 000	6
less than 20 000	20
less than 30 000	46
less than 40 000	65
less than 50 000	72
less than 60 000	77
less than 70 000	80

b See graph

Annual business mileage of 80 sales people

c An estimate for the median is 28 000.

d The interquartile range is 17 000 miles.

e 12 sales people got the increased mileage payments.

2 a

Hours per week	Number of students	Cumulative frequency
0 to less than 15	0	0
15 to less than 20	2	2
20 to less than 25	8	10
25 to less than 30	13	23
30 to less than 35	15	38
35 to less than 40	12	50
40 to less than 45	6	56
45 to less than 50	4	60

b

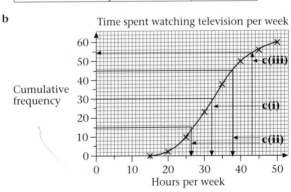

Time spent watching television per week

c i Median = 32 hours   ii Interquartile range = 12 hours
iii Number of students who watch television for more
than 43 hours = 6

Practice exam question

1 a

Time, t (hours)	Number of cars	Cumulative frequency
$0 \leqslant t < 1$	15	15
$1 \leqslant t < 2$	25	40
$2 \leqslant t < 4$	30	70
$4 \leqslant t < 6$	10	80
$6 \leqslant t < 9$	8	88
$9 \leqslant t < 12$	2	90

Time that cars were parked in a car park

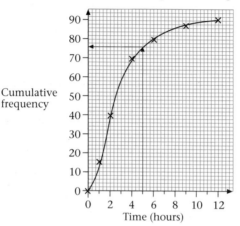

b The number of cars parked for more than five hours is
about 16.

10 Box plots

Practice questions

1

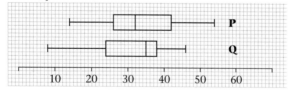

Interquartile range for P is larger than interquartile range for
Q. So the middle 50% of the data is more spread out in P.
The median for Q is larger than the median for P.
2 a Minimum = 16; Lower quartile = 25; Median = 30;
Upper quartile = 38; Maximum = 45
b

Lengths of leaves (mm)

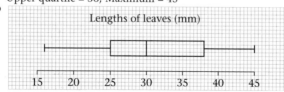

c Range = 29; Interquartile range = 13
3 Answers depend upon data collected.

Practice exam question

1 a

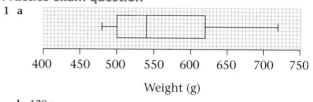

Weight (g)

b 120 g
c i 0   ii 20

11 Moving averages

Practice question 1

1 Gas bills = 4 point; Cinema attendance = 7 point; Student
enrolment = 3 point; Mobile phone bills = 12 point; Shop
sales = 5 point; Council rates = 2 point

Practice questions 2

1 a

Year	Term	Absences from school	Moving average
9	Autumn	20	
	Spring	12	15.3
	Summer	14	16.7
10	Autumn	24	17.3
	Spring	14	18.7
	Summer	18	20.7
11	Autumn	30	21.3
	Spring	16	22.3
	Summer	21	

b, c

Jimmy's absences from school

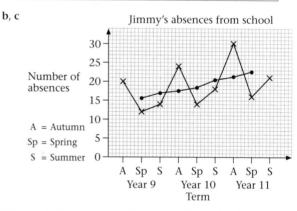

A = Autumn
Sp = Spring
S = Summer

d Jimmy's absence gradually increased over the three years.
It was always the highest in the autumn term.

2 a see graph **b** 4 point moving average

Year	2001				2002			
Quarter	Q1	Q2	Q3	Q4	Q1	Q2	Q3	Q4
Charge (£)	50	55	61	62	58	64	69	75
Moving average			57	59	61.25	63.25	66.5	

c see graph **d** see graph
e Average seasonal component is 3.75. Estimate for trend at Q1 2003 is 72. Estimate for telephone charge for Q1 2003 is £68.25.

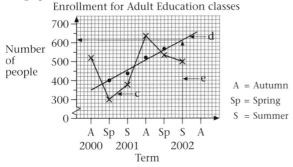

Quarterly telephone charges

Practice exam question

1 a 400
b There are three terms in a year.
c see graph **d** 440; 520; 560

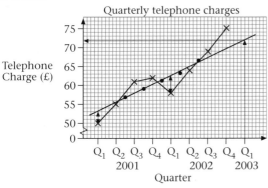

Enrollment for Adult Education classes

A = Autumn
Sp = Spring
S = Summer

e 610 **f** 790

12 Mean of a discrete frequency distribution

Practice questions
1 2.15 **2** 24.46

Practice exam question
1 3.35

13 Grouped data

Practice questions 1
1 4.8 letters **2** 13.6 m

Practice questions 2
1 a 6 kg to less than 7 kg **b** 4–6 letters **c** $0.0 < x \le 10.0$ m
2 a 10–20 **b** 20–25 **c** 2–3

Practice questions 3
1 a 18 **b** 1

Practice questions 4
1 a 5 kg to less than 6 kg **b** 10.0 m $< x \le 20.0$ m
  c 14.0 s $< t \le 15.0$ s
2 10–19 words

Practice exam questions
1 14.24 s **2** 1 houshold **3** 11–20 words

14 Comparing data

Practice questions
1 a The range of the Ripe reds means that the largest Ripe reds are larger than the largest King toms.
  b King toms have a higher mean, so on average the size of the tomatoes is bigger.
2 The average mark (median) for Science is lower than the average mark for English. The range for science is greater than the range for English, i.e. the Science results are more spread out.

Practice exam questions
1 a The mean diameter of the lettuces planted by hand is larger than those planted by machine showing that on average the lettuces planted by hand are larger.
  b The interquartile range of the lettuces planted by machine is smaller than that of the lettuces planted by hand. This shows that the lettuces planted by machine are more consistent in size.
2 a

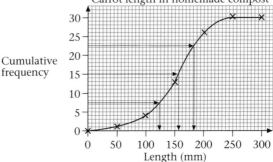

Carrot length in homemade compost

b Median = 160 mm; Interquartile range 56 mm
c

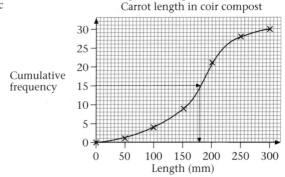

Carrot length in coir compost

d The median for the carrots grown in coir compost (175 mm) is larger than the median for the carrots grown in homemade compost (156 mm). This suggests that on average carrots grown in coir compost are larger.

Answers

15 Single events

Practice questions

1 a $\frac{1}{6}$ b $\frac{1}{6}$ c $\frac{1}{2}$ d $\frac{1}{2}$ e $\frac{1}{2}$ f 0

2 a $\frac{1}{52}$ b $\frac{1}{52}$ c $\frac{1}{52}$ d $\frac{1}{26}$ e $\frac{1}{13}$ f $\frac{3}{13}$ g $\frac{10}{13}$ h $\frac{1}{2}$

Practice exam questions

1 a A: about 0.5, B: above 0.8, C: between 0.1 & 0.3
 b A
 c A standard six-sided dice landing on number 7.
 d A two-headed coin will land on heads.

16 Outcomes for two successive events

Practice questions

1 a

First child	Second child	Third child
B	B	B
B	B	G
B	G	B
B	G	G
G	B	B
G	B	G
G	G	B
G	G	G

b $\frac{1}{8}$ c $\frac{3}{8}$

2 a

	Dice 1					
	1	2	3	4	5	6
1	2	3	4	5	6	7
2	3	4	5	6	7	8
3	4	5	6	7	8	9
4	5	6	7	8	9	10
5	6	7	8	9	10	11
6	7	8	9	10	11	12

(Dice 2 labels rows)

b i $\frac{1}{9}$ ii 7 c 5

Practice exam question

1 a

		Dice					
		1	2	3	4	5	6
Coin	Tails	2	4	6	8	10	12
	Heads	1	2	3	4	5	6

b $\frac{1}{12}$ c $\frac{7}{12}$

17 Mutually exclusive events

Practice question

1 0.75

Practice exam question

1 a 0.55 b 0.30

2 a $\frac{8}{20}$ b 120 c $\frac{12}{17}$ d A and C are not mutually exclusive.

18 Tree diagrams

Practice exam questions

1 a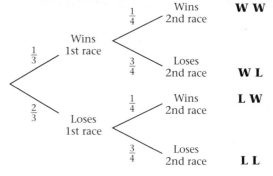

b $\frac{1}{12}$ c $\frac{5}{12}$

2 a Mrs Choudbury buying card

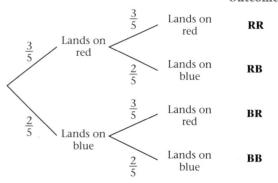

b 0.56

3 a Greg spins a spinner

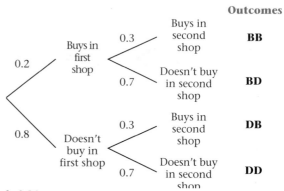

c $\frac{9}{25}$

19 Comparing experimental and theoretical probability

Practice questions

1 a $\frac{9}{20}$ b $\frac{11}{20}$ c $\frac{1}{2}$ d $\frac{1}{2}$

2 a Method A b Method C c Method D

Practice exam questions

1 a Method B b Method A c Method C d Method D
2 a Method C b Method A c Method D
3 a 0.91 b i $\frac{3}{25}$ ii The sample is not as large.

20 Relative frequency

Practice questions

1 a 1 b 6 c 6 d 10 e 10
2 a

Number of spins	10	20	50	100
Number of times the spinner lands on red	3	8	15	32
Relative frequency of landing on red	0.3	0.4	0.3	0.32

b 0.32 because this is based on the largest amount of trials done in the experiment.

Practice exam questions

1 a $\frac{2}{5}$ b i 0.4 ii 0.45 c $\frac{19}{100}$

2 a 8 b No, as the result for 15 spins is not known.
  c It approaches 0.33 $\left(\frac{1}{3}\right)$. d i 2 ii $\frac{1}{9}$

Practice exam paper

Section A

1 a

	1	2	3	4	5	6
1	2	3	4	5	6	7
2	3	4	5	6	7	8
3	4	5	6	7	8	9
4	5	6	7	8	9	10
5	6	7	8	9	10	11
6	7	8	9	10	11	12

b i $P(6) = \frac{5}{36}$
  ii 7
  iii 10
c 10

2 a

Eye colour	Number of students	Angle (°)
Blue	252	168
Brown	126	84
Green	108	72
Hazel	54	36

3 a
```
0 | 6 7 8
1 | 3 4 7 9
2 | 0 2 5 6
```
Key: 1 | 3   represents 13 passengers

b 8 c 17 d 18
4 27 years

Section B

5 a $\frac{1}{4}$ b $\frac{5}{12}$ c $\frac{2}{3}$

6 a b

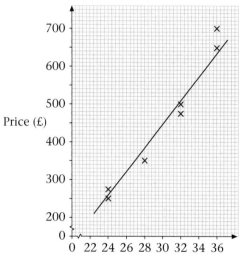

c The larger the screen size the greater the price.
d 42 inches is outside the plotted data so correlation may not continue.
7 540
8 a i Median = 65 ii Interquartile range = 7
  b 38 cars
  c

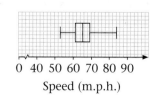

Speed (m.p.h.)

Order Form

Firm Orders – please add quantity required in 'Order Qty' column. **To obtain an Approval Copy** – please tick the relevant 'A' box(es). Where a tick box is shaded this option is not available.

Intermediate

Order Qty	A		ISBN	Title
____	☐	(1)	0 582 79593 1	AQA GCSE Maths Intermediate Module 1
____	☐	(2)	0 582 79594 X	AQA GCSE Maths Intermediate Module 3
____	☐	(3)	0 582 79595 8	AQA GCSE Maths Intermediate Module 5

Higher

Order Qty	A		ISBN	Title
____	☐	(4)	0 582 79596 6	AQA GCSE Maths Higher Module 1
____	☐	(5)	0 582 79597 4	AQA GCSE Maths Higher Module 3
____	☐	(6)	0 582 79598 2	AQA GCSE Maths Higher Module 5

GCSE Maths Exam Tutor and the Coursework Companion

Order Qty	A		ISBN	Title
____	☐	(7)	0 582 79599 0	GCSE Maths Coursework Companion
____	☐	(8)	0 582 82262 9	GCSE Maths Tutor Intermediate Workbook & CD ROM
____	☐	(9)	0 582 82264 5	GCSE Maths Tutor Higher Workbook & CD ROM
____	☐	(10)	0 582 82266 1	GCSE Maths Tutor Intermediate Site License
____	☐	(11)	0 582 82267 X	GCSE Maths Tutor Higher Site License

Call 0800 579 579 or visit www.longman.co.uk
to check the price of each component

TOTAL [   ]

SCHOOL DETAILS (Please use BLOCK capitals)

Mr/Mrs/Miss/Ms/Dr _____

School _____

_____

Position _____

Address _____

_____

Postcode _____

Telephone No _____

REFERENCE CODE ED03-76   (Please quote when ordering)

Choose the most convenient way to pay:

☐   I enclose a cheque for £ _____
    made payable to *Pearson Education Limited*.

☐   Please invoice me
    My school order number is _____ .

FOR CREDIT CARD ORDERS, please call our Schools Enquiry Line FREE on 0800 579 579, Reference Code ED03-76.

Signature _____   Date _____

To receive your FREE e-newsletter containing the latest information on free resources and special offers please register at www.longman.co.uk

Complete and return this form or a photocopy to our FREEPOST address: Secondary Marketing Department, Schools Division, Longman, FREEPOST ANG2041, HARLOW, Essex, CM20 2YF. No stamp required if posted in the UK. Alternatively phone FREE on 0800 579 579 quoting Reference Code ED03-76.